Soul Afterlife

Beyond the Near-Death Experience

Soul Afterlife

Beyond the Near-Death Experience

Bud Megargee

Published by: KDP—Kindle Direct Publishing

CONTENTS

AUTHOR'S NOTE

As luck would have it, for the duration of my life, I have securely stored all my life imprints—the triumphs, disappointments, warnings, and blemishes—for safekeeping. One thing that I cannot warehouse, however, is my unanswered questions, and at the top of that list is this: What happens when this life comes to an end?

Here is something that I seldom talk about: during stolen moments of meditative reflection, I often become aware of the actions that drive how I view the aftereffects of my life. Every so often, I develop an uneasiness about all of this. This unease hinges on the muffled thoughts that seem to connect with my built-in stability—something that I am not always in touch with. In these moments, I struggle to exchange my newly meditative calm for everyday human awareness. Despite this tussle, I inevitably come to realize that there are serious questions about the purpose of my life and the possibility of a soul life hereafter.

I would like to think that a desire to find answers to these questions might offer a thoughtful approach to the existence of an afterlife—a soul life that is architecturally designed to balance out my ego's need for continuance. My thoughts on this matter? Maybe if I could construct an expedition into the realm of souls with an optimistic viewpoint, the possibility of clarity, mindfulness, awareness, and, in the end, purposefulness, would exist.

Being human, I am inherently calibrated to experience some separation between what I have been taught and how those learnings relate to my human experience—my lifelong conditioning. This gives me the ability to proclaim that I am unconditionally able to distinguish between the real and the unreal. As a writer, however, I approach this afterlife conundrum with questions, and the desire to know that there is a deeper understanding to be had about life's mystical puzzles. Specifically, when I die, is there some type of continuation, and if so, what does that look like?

As a result, what follows is an intimate, interactive, and Socratic-like journal that explores the possible aspects of an otherworldly soul life. My interest focuses on the existence of both human and spiritual energies that, time and again, reside in the untraveled hallways of life.

There are occasions when the journey to answer metaphysical questions requires the assistance of others, who have unorthodox skills. To gain this assistance, I traveled to the rural, mountainous community of Berwick, Pennsylvania, as I have throughout my multiyear voyage, to seek the partially voice-channeled assistance of Shirlet Enama. This oddly talented and bold oracle has the capacity to see and contact spirit/soul guides from the "other side." I have worked with this individual before, and it is through this relationship that I have the ability to compare my academic and Buddhist teachings with spiritual schoolings through souls who know me better than I know myself. In doing so, it may be possible to examine and resolve the questions I have about the continuation of the consciousness that I understand to be Bud Megargee.

As I have stated throughout my unworldly excursions, it is not my intention to convince anyone of one unique spiritual or religious belief over another—especially regarding what may transpire following our lives. Rather, what follows is simply a continuation of my spiritual learning experience and pursuit to find answers to seemingly unanswerable questions.

All the resulting dialogues are not intended to validate the existence of soulful monks, spirit guides, or otherworldly energies. I am unpretentiously asking nontraditional questions and, in doing so, pressing up against the boundaries of my long-established spiritual beliefs.

INTRODUCTION

For a time, I studied Eastern philosophy, specifically, the concept of "no self/no soul" (the Theravada Buddhist doctrine of anatman), to better understand if there is a continuation of my soul when I pass. During that period, I had planned on taking a secretive journey into a world that would question the basic understanding of my conventional Catholic schooling.

Initially, I had hoped to take this expedition underground, by way of an unaccompanied mission. At the eleventh hour, I considered getting in touch with a guide willing to work with an ambitious author who was trying to catalog his mystical voyage—someone whom I felt comfortable and confident around to entrust with my cross-questioning beliefs.

The reason for my change of heart? I believed that my whole endeavor could be plagued with various levels of indisputable uncertainty—psychologically, socially, spiritually, and from a story-bound perspective. In any case, I suspected that there would be unique challenges in trying to put into coherent words a transcendent experience that I anticipated being both ineffable and otherworldly.

Fervent curiosity might be what best described the motivation I felt as I began exploring how "no self/no soul" might affect my thoughts about life after death and the path a soul might experience. All things considered, I read as much as I could involving the research into near-death experiences (NDEs). But I expected that there might be more. I tried to picture something beyond extraordinary.

To launch this undertaking, I devoted many hours to visiting with Shirlet Enama—the exclusive and sought-after psychic/oracle residing in the mountainous region of Berwick, Pennsylvania. My charge to her? Simply to help me examine the complexities of soul life.

This individual has worked with me in the past on multiple nonfiction writings involving the soul and quickly became a supportive escort, capable of channeling Laz, an important personal soul guide who could offer an unconventional understanding of life after death.

Throughout this time, I talked to many people about the possible life of a soul. Most were hand-raising believers of one religious faith or another. Yet, despite their accepted code of conviction, several underwent "mystical experiences" that left them with the unshakable conviction that there was something more to life after death than they had come to accept as true, leaving them with a personal feeling that the next world might be more intricate than any of us might have envisioned.

Not everything that I heard from these individuals made me eager to follow them down their private rabbit holes. After all, I have never been one for deep, nonstop introspection. Generally, I would rather leave my personal psychic depths undisturbed—choosing instead to allow someone like Shirlet Enama to walk down those darkened stairs—and truthfully, there is quite enough for me to deal with during the light of day. I had come to believe that all the material regarding the world of a soul's interior had been stowed away for a reason, and unless I was looking for something specific to help solve a worldly issue, why would any untrained individual like myself go into a pitch-black basement and switch on those lights?

Every so often, in the early morning hours of restless nights, I toss myself into an outburst of worry so unstable that the wheels appear to come off my carriage. At such times, I begin to seriously entertain the possibility that somewhere deep beyond my easygoing existence there subsists a vagueness made up of forces that are more than I can understand. These mysteries seem to rest just below the exterior of my understanding and leave me with this question: When I pass, what becomes of me—the consciousness and personality I understand to be Bud Megargee? Does it stay intact? These are the moments when I wonder, do I really want to find out?

During my graduate studies, a psychology professor stated that there are three things that have the capacity to create a self-imposed loss of emotional control: other people, the complexity of our own minds, and what happens after we die. Put me down for all three—but there are times when my curiosity gets the best of me. Such a time has arrived. A time to become more open to the possibility that my human ego might not be as absolute as I would like.

I accept that many historical beliefs turn into academic or philosophical challenges—some becoming discredited in their entirety. But I trust that expeditions of uncertainty are

human travels into confusing and often ambiguous passage-
ways with the intention of examining all possibilities, not just
our time-honored institutional conditioning. This is just such
a voyage.

Two final comments are in order before we start. First, in
what follows, I have at times changed or removed the names
of people who have shared critical moments with me. Unless
they gave me permission to use their names or the locations
of events, I chose to protect their privacy.

Finally, I caution readers that these Socratic-like dialogues
are not intended to demean or undermine any person's beliefs,
religious or otherwise. They are meant only to catalog my
personal journey of spiritual self-discovery. There are many
paths to the truth—this is merely a continuation of mine.

CHAPTER 1

The Octopus Analogy

Over an eight-year period, I have been an accessory to many unimaginable stories involving the world of spirits, and the subplots of these moments did not always occur in a conventional fashion.

While researching the otherworldly aspects of nonphysical realities, I became conscious of uncommon analogies and how they are used. My thoughts? Analogies are not just stories in the sense of being entertainment—they are powerful tools for teaching, complete with a situation and purpose. In the end, some of these mystical narratives are profound, some can be marginal, but none was more complex or influential than the octopus analogy.

I was first introduced to the full complexity of the octopus analogy while working on *Soul Mechanics: Unlocking the Human Warrior* along with Shirlet Enama and the channeled soul guide Laz. Knowing that any future discussion regarding an afterlife would likely resurrect that spiritual teaching tool, I reasoned that a serviceable explanation of the octopus analogy might be helpful.

As a starting point, hearing about the world of souls within the framework of a sea creature was clearly odd. I felt bowled over, like I had become part of a shaken New York City snow globe. Yet, as time passed and more material was made known, the comparison became plausible.

Mysteriously, whenever I encounter a dramatic departure from my typical religious or spiritual teachings, I tend to fast-forward to the outcomes of those complex teaching/learning moments, skipping over the journey that led me to them. Sometimes, when it is meticulousness that matters most, I need to pause and rewind the tape. I believe that grasping the fine points of this analogy is such a moment. Here is a brief example.

Apparently, when a soul is born, it binds together with others in a small cluster, with four, five, or six souls essentially forming their initial "learning groups." These souls are intimate and the act of spiritual mates coming together is the creation of what is referred to within the analogy as the octopus's head.

Souls join in a cluster for a variety of reasons, but at the top of the list is the need for spiritual adventure and advancement—to learn the practical application of what is already known but not experienced. To accomplish this, each soul fragments, like cutting a diamond, and incarnations (or the octopus's appendages) are dropped by each clustered soul, with the objective of focusing on the details of a specific life-learning issue (for example, healing or teaching).

At this point, I need to stop briefly. A detailed explanation of this concept is important to understanding an afterlife journey. Yet to go any further might cause unintended misperceptions.

For the sake of accuracy, I took the extraordinary step of asking my soul guide Laz to explain his interpretation of the octopus analogy a second time. My hope is that he will agree.

Bud: Laz, would you take a moment and shed light on what is behind the octopus analogy? For example, to start, what is the intention of a soul being assigned to a cluster group?

Laz: Very simply—it is a method of management. There are so many souls in existence that forming into clusters allows for great variation to take place. Plus, they are more easily managed if they are in groups. It is also a way for different souls to connect. For example, some groups can stay together for multiple lifetimes and, in doing so, create amazingly learning relationships.

B: Can you explain more about this?

L: You have a group of souls who go through incarnations, sometimes together, and they are formed into an energy-supported cluster. When an individual soul decides to incarnate, it develops multiple variations of that incarnation because it wishes to learn everything it can from every possible angle. To continue with the analogy, that is when it would drop down several tentacles from the octopus's head, and each tentacle would carry one of the incarnation variables. At that time, because the soul's energy is cut like a diamond, it has the capacity to take on multiple human shells.

I need you to follow this next part, because this is unlike what you have been taught: When each incarnation ends, that portion of the faceted energy does not move directly back to the octopus's head. Rather, it moves within the other tentacles, which are still active, to help the other incarnations complete the learning. The faceted portions of the soul's energy keep attaching to active lives until the soul completes all the incarnations, and only then does it form back into its "higher self" within the head of the octopus. That is when the soul becomes whole again and returns to its cluster companions. Once there, that soul can determine whether it will help guide its mates with their incarnations, reincarnate itself, or advance to a higher soul cluster. Additional options are available for more advanced souls. They may choose to become descendants and decide to oversee and guide lesser-developed cluster groups. From my perspective, it is quite simple—it is all about learning.

B: What occurred for souls to form into a cluster in the first place? Was it a similarity of personality or just a general selection?

L: That union was made many lifetimes ago for a wide variety of reasons.

B: Can you explain a little further? As an example—the souls in my cluster group, did they have similar or different personalities?

L: Each soul is required to do a lot of work to join with a cluster group. You don't just arrive at the head of an octopus by chance. You must manage, through many lifetimes, to develop yourself as a soul to get to the point where you can move from head to head indiscriminately.

B: Laz, before I became a member within the head of my current octopus, was I operating as an independent soul?

L: Not necessarily—you could have been a member of a less-developed cluster group.

B: A soul is always part of a group—large or small?

L: Yes.

B: And as they mature, develop, and evolve, they move into other groups that are more compatible?

L: Yes.

B: For a moment, take me back to the beginning: When souls are born, are they put into a cluster that is appropriate for their level of vibration—the frequency of their energy?

L: Yes. Additionally, in the beginning, you are in only one incarnation, and you are at the very distant tip of the farthest tentacle of your first octopus. As you move through each new incarnation and up each tentacle, you advance more and more. The more advanced, the more frequently your cluster group is likely to be modified or change to accommodate your newly developed frequency.

   The point that you may be missing is that each "soul member" of the cluster has incarnated into its learning labs, as you have. Like I suggested about tentacles' lives, when that soul energy passes from one of its incarnations, it does not immediately return to a position within the head of the octopus. Unlike the movement of soul energy between its own incarnations, it is doubtful that soul energy will attach to one of the other soul cluster members.

B: This can be very confusing. In the past, you have suggested that many of the souls currently on this planet are young souls, and that they might have been part of a limited number of incarnations or clusters. Is that an accurate statement?

L: Yes.

B: These young souls would have had a smaller number of learning tentacles dropped from their octopuses' heads?

L: Yes.

B: A soul individually sets out initial learning paths in a small number of learning episodes?

L: Yes, and the further developed you are as a soul, the larger the number of tentacles that are dropped, and the more diverse or split your soul is for learning. You are in a position of distributing small amounts of your soul energy to each incarnation, yet you are expected to learn twice as much. The younger souls are applying greater amounts of energy to a smaller number of incarnations, thereby giving themselves a better chance to learn.

B: Laz, I know that we are likely to expand on all of this, but for next time, what should we concentrate on as we begin the journey into the afterlife?

L: It would be important to understand the immediate effect that the seven soul senses have upon passing and how that relates to soul fragmentation. This is going to be a test; it will directly confront your current belief system. It is extraordinarily unlike anything you learned from your near-death understandings.

I believe that I have already crossed the Rubicon and reached a point of no return with my afterlife journey. In committing to a specific course of action by revisiting the octopus analogy, I have one question: Have I exposed a great source of unexpected information, or have I simply foreshadowed what is to come?

In leaping over the walls of conventional reasoning, there seems to be something in my innate mental toolbox that stubbornly refuses to give up on seeking substitute portrayals of an afterlife, even if it is in my best interest and would preserve my sanity to do so.

The explanation that my soul's existence might be generated from the cluster group and calculated from numerous lifetimes is equally mesmerizing and terrifying. If this is accurate and my soul energy has the capacity to facet like a diamond and "roll over" to alternative incarnations, then how I perceive my human ego—that which I understand to be Bud Megargee—is forever to be altered.

In trying to understand an afterlife puzzle, it is often impossible for me to perceive all the relative elements directly. As a result, I must trust that my otherworldly gathered information is built upon the backs of assigned proxies or other specialized resources. With mysterious questions of the hereafter as my story line backdrop, Shirlet and Laz are ultimately my only translators.

Amazingly, the introduction of the octopus analogy is only the beginning of this journey. Part of my reasoning for plunging into the world of souls is my need to make sense of all the uncommon outcomes that a nonphysical world traveler is likely to bump into. In my eagerness to ask questions, perhaps my motivation has always been to isolate my unusual questioning of unfamiliar situations. In doing so, I may be quietly supporting a constructive assessment of what I genuinely accept as true. Maybe that is what I really want to bring into the open.

There is certain to be an expansion on this analogy as I rummage deeper into the world of souls, but for now, I am curious about the seven senses. This is a new concept to me and has not been discussed in any research or readings I have conducted to date. I suspect that I am about to submerge further into unfamiliar waters.

CHAPTER 2

The Soul's Seven Senses

On a warm fall day in the early seventies, I, along with a small group of recent psychology graduates, was volunteering at a community crisis clinic located several miles from the King of Prussia exit on the Pennsylvania turnpike.

We were admiring the summerlike weather and local traffic from our front door when the emergency intercom rang. The Pennsylvania state troopers were inbounding with a young male who was found semiconscious on the side of the road. They were indicating via mobile and pager that it was a potential drug overdose.

The clinic was located less than one hundred yards from the local hospital emergency room, where our medical director was a staff physician. As luck would have it, he was on duty. His team was placed on notice, and because I had made the initial call to the ER, he instructed me to accompany the troopers.

Without much notice, the state police vehicle approached the south side of our building, and the trooper who was driving called for me to jump in.

A designated treatment team was waiting at the ER entrance, and while extracting the young man from the vehicle, I noticed the patient's complexion; it was a light shade of blue—he had stopped breathing. I paused for a moment and forced myself not to freeze. Watching a person dying up close was a first for me.

For anyone who has worked around trauma centers, they are magical—a process of adaptive, organized chaos. I remember being dazzled by the synchronicity of events. In this case, there was a flurry of action, and the man conducting all the activity was my medical director. I remember thinking, "These people are amazing."

The state troopers' notes indicated that the young man's name was Whitney and that he had been hitchhiking across the country from California. Unfortunately, he now found himself fighting for every breath in an unfamiliar town, three thousand miles from home.

The attending physician called for the standard overdose protocol—an immediate naloxone HCL (Narcan) injection—and I was amazed at what happened next. In less than a minute, the young man became conscious, looked at everyone in the treatment room, and then commenced to pull out all the tubes that were administering fluids. Predictably, he sat up on the edge of the gurney and announced, with emphasis, "I'm out of here." Placing his stethoscope around his own neck, my medical director looked straight at me and said, "He's all yours."

Fortunately, with the help of the nursing staff, we were able to convince Whitney to stay for the evening by informing him that the Narcan would eventually wear off. I remained at the ER until he was placed in a private room within the hospital tower and promised the staff that I would return later.

I recall this story, not because of the actions that brought Whitney to the emergency room or the therapeutic interventions that followed, but because of the events that transpired later that evening.

When I arrived back at the hospital, Whitney seemed far off and emotionally detached. There was something in his eyes that kept me at a distance—something deep, troubled, intelligent, and dark. This was a young man who did not want to be reached.

Patiently, I sat across from him and waited. I told him I was there only to assist and that if he was not comfortable talking, that would be OK. What I did not expect was what he revealed to me just prior to my leaving.

As I moved toward the door, he quietly uttered, "Do you ever think about dying?" At first, I was taken aback, and I must have had an odd expression because his eyes widened as I responded, "Not very often." Closing his eyes, he whispered, "Are you interested in learning what it is like?"

For an hour and a half, Whitney described what I have come to accept as his near-death experience. His story recall was absolute and animated, and the emotionally laden details rendered a picture as if it were all happening in real time. I was so hypnotized that I failed to take a single note—I just listened.

He expressed, in detail, a liberating physical detachment from the planet, in which he was transfixed by his ability to see and hear everything all at once—it was as though he was on total information overload. He described how he had observed all the ER interventions, including how the people treating him moved about the room. With a wrinkled, confused brow, he tried to express how he was able to monitor his surroundings and yet sail through what he described as a swirling, cloth-like corridor at the same time. Every so often, Whitney would dwell on how the force and rapidity of what he experienced were now affecting his human psyche and the ability to return to a grounded emotional state. In an offbeat way, he was questioning his mental stability.

"It was all so real," he explained as he tried to characterize how he encountered several vaporous figures that were lovingly approaching him but not clearly definable. And finally, I recall that he expressed his surprise at being revived. It was an awakening that caused an emotional disappointment, because while he was "dead," he had finally felt at peace with himself.

As I drove home later, I thought that Whitney's life must have seemed to be blissfully whipping by until his brief encounter with death. And now I believed it would be forever changed.

I am telling this story because it is one of those life experiences that initially appears to be odd and later turns out to be privately retained for future reference. Now, however, as my journey takes me to the outer edges of Whitney's experience, I think more about the evening I spent in Whitney's hospital room.

We lost contact with Whitney after his discharge two days later—he had demanded the discharge. I presume he went back to California, but there was no way to know. What I do know, however, is this: Laz has shared two important aspects of the afterlife that directly relate to Whitney's story.

First, the tunnel is not something that we pass through, like a doorway or passageway to another dimension. It is our aura, our human energy field, spinning at the frequency and vibration formed by the experiences of our current and past lives.

Second, NDEs are not complete examples of a soul's life after death, despite the intermittent pause in our bodily functions. Soul life initiates with a complete disconnection from the human shell. NDEs merely walk along the perimeter of a soul existence. Laz suggests that absolute soul detachment from the human shell is different; it is multifaceted, and what we experience thereafter ranges widely and is extremely complex.

With the injection of those opioid-antagonist chemicals, Whitney apparently avoided the faceting of his energy. Sadly, he was incapable of verifying the existence of an "octopus head." And finally, he was powerless to give a preview of the seven senses of the soul.

I suspect that the seven soul senses are very different from Whitney's brief encounter with the afterlife. I believe I should strap myself in for the ride.

Laz: With tonight's discussion, I could continue with the birth of a soul, but that is not important or what most people need to know.

Shirlet: I would agree, Bud. Most people who visit with me want to know if an afterlife—heaven and so forth—is consistent with their religious beliefs.

Bud: Do they simply want to know, "When I pass, what will I experience?"

S: Yes.

L: It is possible that when you pass, it is your "spiritual thought clearance" that will decide which spiritual door you open and what vibration level you will be operating from.

Remember, the soul is faceted like a diamond, and when you pass, your soul goes into the remaining levels of the octopus, as we previously described. That is the first thing you need to become aware of—your energy will "roll over" to the other incarnations. The soul needs to complete all those lives and the learning that was intended. There will come a time when the last human shell in your octopus tentacle group passes, but before that, your energy—that which you understand to be Bud Megargee—disperses into the seven different senses of existence.

B: I have a reasonable but confused understanding of the soul faceting, but it is not consistent with my spiritual or religious upbringing. I have never heard of the seven soul senses.

L: I understand. When you pass, and a specific learning

octopus tentacle has been completed, the focus becomes the seven soul senses, and every one of them is searching for its own vibration level. Let me go through each one—then we can talk more.

One of the primary senses is love. This soul viewpoint is the part of you that wants to remain in the human vibration field that you developed while living and watch over and protect current loved ones—your children, wife or husband, and so on. Do you understand? Several authors have written about this, and on occasion, people who experience what you call "near death" get a distant glimpse of this sense.

There is an additional soul sense that is called fear. This has a position of concern or worry. As a result, it fosters the possibility of the soul hiding or going to a realm that is perceived as more comfortable. It retreats to a more comfortable place, similar to living in its human shell.

A third sense is identified as peace. This part of the soul desires a higher vibration level than it achieved during the human incarnation. It is contemplating a reincarnation into a new human life, or it may wish to remain stationary and heal from the wounds that it has experienced in its earthly incarnation. The road chosen depends on the frequency that was attained while living.

The fourth sense, which is important for you to know, is hate. This segment of your soul is resentful, angry, revengeful, and sick of things. This isn't just you; every human has this sense. It seeks problems or wants to get back at people— and it can because it will have the power. This is not the most attractive portion of the soul, but it could be an answer for some human hauntings.

The fifth sense I will call God or perhaps better stated, a God connection. It is the link that wants to ascend and raise its vibration so as to become a creator in its own right and watch over other people. In a way, with its interest in watching over others, it is trying to become like me.

Now, the sixth faceted sense is the zone of karmic events. This is the aspect of the soul that takes the beatings for all the incidents that were carried out during the last incarnation. This part of human energy can stay on its most recent plane of existence. Additionally, it can stick to individuals who were involved in a specific karmic event or go to a much lower vibration to resolve its karma. This portion of the soul is very powerful and can unite the other facets—essentially having them share in the torment it is experiencing. This is what some consider hell.

The last sense, the seventh, is the most interesting of all the faceted senses. This is the part of the soul that knows about everything—time, the Akashic records, all spiritual planning, past lives, and the map of who you truly are. This is the part of the soul that is the "overseer." It collects every other faceted sense of the soul so that things are not running amok. This segment takes the responsibility to ensure that the other faceted senses pull together and begin the process of formatting for reincarnation. You cannot reincarnate until all the senses have completed the voyage within their specific area of responsibility and come together to make you whole.

B: Are you suggesting that each of the seven senses relates to one of the seven chakras?

L: They only relate to them—they are not directly connected.

B: I have so many questions about all of this. But first, upon passing, the soul does not go to one specific sense but is split into all seven by some percentage of energy or vibration?

L: Remember our diamond analogy. It is as if the soul has been split like a puzzle, and it needs to sort out these experiences so that it can come back together and know its position. You are right—the percentage you reference depends on the vibration level of the soul upon passing.

B: Interesting. Throughout my life, I am exposed to these seven senses, and when I pass, there is a portion of my soul that isolates to each of these areas?

L: Yes, but not as a singular group—as the faceted or diamond portions of your soul. Let me emphasize again: you cannot consider reincarnating until all the senses have explored these areas and are brought back together.

B: What is the simplest way to understand this very radical concept?

L: Say that you are an orb, and you have been cut into sections like a pie. When you pass from this incarnation, the part of you that is love goes to that sense, the part that is peace goes to peace, and so forth—portions of your energy or soul direct themselves to the appropriate sense.

B: Because I have had those seven experiences?

L: Correct.

B: Take me further down this path: Once my energy has been separated into the seven sections of the "pie," what happens?

L: You live in an existence within those seven different "senses" until you have been reeled in by the seventh sense and brought back together as the energy that you understand to be Bud Megargee.

B: Exactly what must occur within each of those six "senses" for the seventh sense to bring all the energy back together?

L: Each sense must live out its connection as a soul, not as a human.

B: Within the spirit world?

L: Yes. It is not my intention to confuse you any more than I already have, but your questions might answer why there are so many hauntings. That is why some souls are seen after they pass, and others are not. Some are working out these require-ments and are drifting into the human realm.

B: I believe I am getting closer to understanding: you live out the connections or experiences as a soul within the vibrational level that you have achieved while a living human.

L: Yes.

B: Is that why you have emphasized the importance of attend-ing to my spiritual vibration while living? Because if I am operating at a higher vibration, I would be in any one of the six senses for shorter periods of time?

L: Essentially, yes. However, what you describe as time is of no importance here. The higher the vibration, the quicker the voyage. For some, like many monks, it is a blink of an eye. Others, from a lower vibration, cannot comprehend anything that they see, and sadly, movement takes a longer period.

B: Laz, what relationship does this have to the different di-mensions or universes that you have discussed in the past? Can the soul's energy, within one of the seven senses, resolve its issues in alternative dimensions?

L: Yes. An obligation that is not human is no longer a hu-man obligation. Only your shell is here to address the human obligation. When the shell passes and the soul is disconnected from its prior obligation, the human interest is removed.

B: Let's slow down for a second. Once I have completed my octopus-incarnation responsibilities, what is the first thing that I experience? Is it the splitting of my soul into the seven senses? And if so, is that traumatic?

L: For some, the answer is yes. Others experience it as a release—a great release from being in a tight space and finally free from it.

B: And is my consciousness or ego aware that I have been split into these sections?

L: Your consciousness only experiences the sense that you are in at that time. Each portion of your consciousness is experiencing only that area. Lower-vibration human egos have a difficult time comprehending that.

B: I can't imagine what it would be like to have what I consider to be myself split into multiple sections.

L: Let me give you some additional insight. If Shirlet passed, what she would understand, including the separation of consciousness, is dependent on her very high vibration level. If it were not as high, she would experience a great deal of confusion.

B: So, as an example, if her vibration is ninety on a scale of one hundred, most of her energy would be gravitating to the seventh sense—the overseer?

L: Absolutely. But let me introduce one additional important human piece—and I am doing this because you have had an interest in treating people with traumatic experiences during your career. There are times when, as a human, a portion of the soul can split off if it has experienced extreme trauma. Especially if the experience was so bad that the soul cannot comprehend, forgive, or get through it. Part of that soul stays with the living after death—almost like it is trapped. Strangely, this part of the soul remains "lost" until it is brought in by the seventh sense and healed. Then that soul energy is complete and can start considering reincarnation.

S: Wow. I have never heard of this.

L: Shirlet, if this split is not corrected, that would leave an imprinted portion of a soul on earth that did not want to be here. Perhaps these are some of the souls that you see from time to time.

B: To be clear, it is stuck in the spirit realm and only appears on earth to someone with an extremely high vibration level, like Shirlet?

L: Yes. I bring this up only to emphasize again how the energy of a soul has the capacity to segment itself—how powerful it is—and that the human consideration of a soul forever remaining a singular, intact energy field is a false teaching.

B: I would like to think of myself as an average person who has believed that I am one hundred percent of "who I am," and that upon passing, one hundred percent goes to a desired place.

L: That is sad. You would be so wrong, because even while you are living, there is so much more about you to understand; your thinking is not even close to what really happens. It is your human life conditioning, essentially your ego, that keeps your thinking at a lower vibration level.

B: Help me to understand what I often think about: What is the first thing that I will experience upon passing? Is it the tunnel that individuals having an NDE refer to?

L: The simplest explanation is that you leave your shell—it is an exit process. You are exiting at the vibration level that you achieved while living—that is the tunnel; it is that simple. If your octopus-tentacle experience is complete, your soul divides into the senses all at once. Isn't that interesting, how many of you are leaving by splitting?

B: Is this a universal experience for all souls?

L: Hardly. Remember, the tunnel that everyone reads about

is not always an intact energy. It is the aura of the individual spinning at the vibration level that was achieved while living, and sometimes there are negative attachments that slow things down.

B: Are some souls frightened by this different interpretation of passing?

L: That could be the case in some sets of circumstances. It could be fear, maybe confusion—it depends on so many different things.

B: Is it possible that everything that has ever existed is available to the soul who just passed?

L: Yes. Think about this—if all thought creates a solid form, then all thought is available for a passed soul to see or experience as it moves about the seven senses.

B: Can that be the religious understanding of a "life review"?

L: No. It is simply a possible outcome of an experience that may occur if you are at a lower vibration level. Everything that has been thought is available to a soul, and that could be terrifying.

B: If you happen to be at a lower vibration level, how do you find a way through that fog?

L: The best remedy is to have a higher vibration level before you leave the shell as opposed to trying to figure a way out once you are in this fog. You need a high level of vibration to ascend past anything undesirable.

B: I would like to go back to some of my Catholic teachings. If someone believes living a good life is a ticket to heaven, can that happen?

L: Absolutely. You can create your own boundaries and your own world—so to speak—but you will still run into the creations of others. You experience more than just your own creations.

B: And as an example, if a portion of me is in "heaven," would I still experience the other six senses?

L: Yes, and those experiences would be going on at the same time as your experience in heaven. Can you see why the seventh sense must bring everyone back in to form a whole? That part of your energy navigates the trappings within the other six senses.

B: Is there ever a time after the soul splits that I would become aware of the split, and is the overseere communicating with the other six senses to draw every portion of my energy back?

L: Yes. However, if your vibration within each sense is at the same high level, that would ward off any intrusion by other energies.

B: My thoughts keep coming back to the issue of how much time is spent in each sense. Perhaps that is because I do not like the thought of being separated.

L: Time is not a state of being on this side. There is no time, so I could never give you an idea of how long something would take—especially this. Things vary and often depend on the soul's vibration level and advancement through the lifetimes of learning. It would also depend on the frequencies of karmic debt.

B: Laz, how would you explain this discussion in its simplest terms?

L: Hmm. It is an extension of the soul's conscious mind. That is what we have been talking about and what is not traditionally taught. Think about what you have been taught by your Buddhist friends—like they have said, you are more than you think you are.

B: Yes. It is interesting that, from time to time, you come back to that phrase.

L: If you stop and think about what we have discussed, it does start to answer the questions that many humans have—the questions that they cannot get answered because they think that the answer is going to be one individualized statement of all things conveyed upon them through religious doctrine;

however, it is totally out of the realm of that. In the ancient days, some of the great kings and certainly the Egyptians knew about the parting of the soul, and they did attempt to have people try to separate the soul while they were conscious. They knew that the soul had the capacity to split and wanted their consciousness to control it.

B: And the purpose of this?

L: To bring back all the things they needed to know so that they could have the evidence. To bring back the secret of eternal life.

B: Fascinating.

L: If someone could take the fragmented portions of the soul and learn from them before coming back into a whole new life, think of the knowledge that could be gained. It would be shocking. Could the human mind even take it?

B: I am left with this thought: if I believe what you say and have an awareness of this discussion, then I could work on my vibration to avoid being trapped in any of the senses for a protracted period.

L: Yes. Think of it this way—think of a web as high as Mount Everest and down to the deepest portions of the ocean, made up of nothing but extremities that people have thought up and created, all operating at a lower vibrational level. Now think of a soul passing and disconnecting and fragmenting into that web. If this occurred, how far and how soon do you think it can be retrieved from that mess? In a case like this, it is difficult for the segmented portions to even find one another.

B: Are you suggesting that if your vibration or frequency is at a certain level, you could leap over this web?

L: That is your learning for tonight. You need the right inner workings to ascend, meaning your spiritual development is high enough to go through all we discussed tonight—quickly, like it doesn't exist. You must be nimbler than a spider.

One last thing before we stop. You have been reading about near-death experiences. They are just that, near death. The reason no one has reported on all we have discussed is because these individuals did not die. They always returned to the human shell. They may experience a different vibration level or a thought form that they created, but they are still coming back to a human shell—meaning that the soul does not fragment, and they are intact as one form of energy. Once a soul fragments, then you are dead.

B: Why would some report seeing images of people and so forth?

L: Why wouldn't they? They are always around you; Shirlet knows this, and so do the animals. When you are out of your shell, temporarily or otherwise, your spiritual eyes are wide open. Don't misread this—there are times when souls close to them try to meet up with them and escort them or help them ascend, mostly anticipating that the parting soul might be at a lower vibration level.

B: This is a lot to think about. How will we expand on this next time?

L: Let me leave you with this because I know many will be confused about the splitting of the soul and the loss of ego identity. Think about being in a rainstorm and every drop of rain in the town where you live being part of your soul—that is how everything begins; that is how your soul splits.

To build on what we have already discussed, I would like to talk about what breath really is and the role it plays.

I believe we tend to think more in terms of what we are doing and less in terms of who we are becoming.

You might want to think of it this way: We live within a defined circle of life. That which shapes the circle around us is made up of things that we see and things that we do not see, things that may be described and things that are beyond all power of description. It is also made up of things that we may do and things that we may never do. Yes and no each has its proper place in the shaping of the circle, and if the circle is to remain unbroken, we must have complete awareness of every part of it. It is the awareness of the circle's elements that brings out our sense of being, to who we are becoming.

My Buddhist friends believe that our nature is that of a wave—sometimes we are the wave, but we are never separated from the ocean (inter-existence). That we come and go in many appearances, having been transformed by our life experiences. That everything in the world comes into existence in response to cause and effect—that nothing exists in absolute independence of other things or arises of its own accord. Traditional Japanese culture refers to this as *Inga*—literally translated as "destiny" or "fate."

I often leave these sittings internally at odds with what I have learned. Fortunately, the process of transcribing the audiotapes behaves as a filter for me—it amputates the internal conflict I walk away with and allows for welcome awareness.

Here is an example of that awareness. In many ways, the soul's seven senses give emphasis to the responsibility and consequences that are attached to my thoughts, words, and actions. They highlight that my lifelong interactions are the only worldly belongings that convey to the spirit world. My earthly dealings are the ground on which I stand while breathing—but the aftereffects of those actions are somehow securely preset to each of these seven layered senses.

Karma is a word occasionally used to describe human events. Some think it describes "fate" or some form of cosmic justice. In fact, karma is a Sanskrit word that, when properly translated, means "action." Within a Theravada Buddhist community, karma has an even more specific meaning; it is a label capable of explaining all of life's volitional actions.

On the face of it, the dialogue on the soul's seven senses has given me a lot to analyze, and admittedly, it is "out there." Yet in its simplest form, I am at ease with the notion that when a soul embarks on an afterlife journey, it is merely meeting the fruits of its human karmic actions. My self-willed acts— what I choose to say, think, and create—produces an energy vibration that sets into motion the laws of cause and effect. And adjacent to that is every achievable timetable needed to climb above what I have amassed.

At present, I am increasingly sensitive to the idea that my ego and personality may not continue permanently intact following my death. To be more precise, that I may fold into a larger energy entity—one in which I am only a small fraction. For now, I can't yet come to terms with that fact.

It is hard for me to envision what connection breath has with the seven senses—or the octopus analogy, for that matter. My only assurance is that I am likely to experience another eye-opener.

CHAPTER 3

The Source of Breath

In anticipation of meeting with both Shirlet and Laz, I have been thinking about the general function of breathing and how that may relate to our next discussion. As a practicing Buddhist, I understand the role that breath plays in bringing one's reflective process to the current moment.

As basic element of meditation, breath is an expedient object to focus attention on because it is available to everyone. Our breath's gentle in-and-out movement has a natural ability to calm the mind. Concentrating on breathing can be the first step in drawing attention away from the outward commotion that influences our lives and, consequently, the way that we think about the world.

While exploring contemplative psychology, I was encouraged to focus my awareness on how numerous mental states cause noticeable changes in breathing patterns. For example, when I am calm, my breath is long, slow, and gentle, and when I am excited, it becomes short and fast. Further, when I hold my breath in expectation or sigh with sadness or neglect, there are obvious visible changes. Intensely watching the movement of breathing can be part of what leads me to become aware of the fluid movements within my mind. Any mindfulness integration of my breathing, in effect, reinforces how I am balanced in life.

The awareness of the subtleties and the intentionality of breathing can develop into a wonderful lifelong tool. As my appreciation becomes stronger and more refined and its familiarity seamless, is it possible that the barriers to being aware of my soul's purpose may start to dissipate simply by understanding the real purpose of breath? Perhaps that is where Laz will take this.

Laz: The last time we were together, I told you that the splitting of the soul is like rain. Let's go back to that and see if you paid attention to what I was trying to teach. The soul is like rain—that means it is of water. So, what would water be?

Bud: You once told me that water is life.

L: And?

B: Are you searching for the fact that it has electrical or energy features?

L: It does, but that is not where I was going with my question. What else does it have?

B: It can change form?

L: Yes—it has movement, and the soul is like water, so the soul would have many different attributes, including movement. Why wouldn't the soul be able to change into any form it desired or be in any energy field that it desired? It has the capacity to take the form that is needed at that moment. The soul is movement—the soul is existence—the soul is life. Think about this: It has movement, existence, and life—they are all one concept. So, what is the purpose of life? Please answer that for me.

B: I would have preferred an easier question. Could it be to learn?

L: No. Try again.

B: To be?

L: In a way, that is correct, but what I am looking for is *existence is breath*. Now, what connects breath to existence, life, and movement?

B: The natural elements of the earth?

L: That is part of it, but what connects it? Let me help. What connects it is form. Without form, you have no body. Breath creates the body—I am talking about the beginning of time. Breath needs to be given to life to create a form. The soul is movement; it is consciousness; it is ever changing. The breath needs to be able to stop the movement to allow for the form of a human, an animal, a tree, or a flower. Think about this: You have water, and it is a river that is flowing very fast. If you want to slow or stop it, you must dam it up, correct?

B: Yes.

L: Think of breath being the dam for the flow of the soul it created. To stop it for one second in time, like the point of a needle, to create a form—it is amazing. When the shell stops, the soul goes back into the river that is all-knowing and all-consuming.

Let me explain further. Something like what we are discussing—it cannot just be that you die and go to heaven or hell, because that is not correct. That is a concept that may be fed to the living, but that is not true. In some circumstances, you may be able to go to a dimensional level for your actions because your vibration is what pulls you there. It is like a vacuum; whatever your vibration is during your lifetime, that is where you will go. However, like water, the soul is always moving, flowing; it is not stagnant. Stagnation only comes with the human shell, and when that occurs, the human ego takes over, stalling out the soul. It is sad, actually—the soul is then in a prison.

B: Interesting. If everything you said is true, then the breath within the human shell, as you describe, becomes the dam that stops the flow.

L: Yes. It is like having a locked door, and the breath is the key. Without breath, you cannot exist as a human. When the soul exits the shell, it goes to the all-flowing consciousness—it is released.

B: The average person knows that if he or she stops breathing, life will end. You are saying, in part, that when you stop breathing, that is when soul life begins.

L: In a way, yes, but here is a caution to that: those who stop breathing without breath stopping on its own can change their frequency, entering into a lower vibration frequency that people would say is a hell. Therefore, breath is frequency, breath is change, breath is like a gear in your shell—without breath, the shell does not exist. Trees breathe, animals breathe, insects breathe, humans breathe—breath is essential for existence. Breath is the total key; it is a lifespan, and if taken care of, it can complete that lifespan so that the shell can shut down when it is supposed to and ascend. If that does not happen, it is like being caught in that gear where the shell just expires, and the breath is thrown out into a lower vibration level.

B: Conversely, if at a higher vibration level, could you appropriately stop your breath when you choose?

L: Yes. It is like the money in your wallet. You need that money to exist, for food, to pay your bills—without money, you would lose your house, your lights, your water. It is the same concept—think of the shell like that. It must have the breath; it is a component; it is all a package deal. Breath has its own consciousness. The breath is its own entity, and the breath is trying to connect to the soul.

B: This may be a wild assumption on my part, but are you alluding to the fact that breath is what we call God?

L: You are listening tonight, aren't you? Yes, because the breath is your life. The soul is connected to breath, but the shell is not.

B: But we think that breath is ours, that we own it.

L: But you do not.

B: I have been reading and talking with Buddhist monks throughout the years, and they often make the comment "I am home," and they make that comment while they focus on their breathing during meditation. Are you suggesting that this is the case—that concentration on breath is a direct connection to the soul's "home"?

L: Yes, and this is what we need to talk about if you really want to know what happens when you pass. I can teach you about the experiences when you pass, but right now, it is important to understand the reality of breath.

B: I am curious: What can you say to someone who, like me, maintains that what you are suggesting diminishes the understanding of a human ego?

L: I find that the best way to explain any of this is with the analogy of a spider's web. We are all connected like that web. Everything is flowing, expanding, and moving. It is all attached along with breath. If you started with this concept, it could get you into a position of understanding. By linking together there is a vibration of life. For example, do you know that all life is a hum?

B: You mean like the sound my mouth can make?

L: Yes, a hum. The monks all know this. That is why they hum—because they connect with this meditation. They do this because life is a hum, and it is a swift way to connect to the vibration of life. Vibration is sound.

B: You mentioned that in *Soul Mechanics: Unlocking the Human Warrior*.

L: The creator of all knew that all components had to be in the breath. The breath was given sound and life. The breath was given sight, taste, and all the senses. So, the breath had to be planted to animate the shell so that it would have everything. It had to have the breath of life.

B: And by breath, you mean that the creator essentially

propelled everything into existence—essentially breathing life into everything?

L: Yes. Think of this: when you are spiraling out of the shell, there is one thing that the soul wants to do besides moving into the other existences of the seven senses—it is always seeking breath.

B: Seeking to accumulate more or to connect to breath?

L: To have it so that the soul can form into a reincarnation position.

B: I was mistaken to think that it needed to acquire more "energy"?

L: No, it is flowing; it is all. Think of having a blueprint of a house. You have it on paper, and you have the money and people to start your project, but you will not have the house itself until it is built. Think of the soul as the blueprint and the breath as the house.

Shirlet: I find that an interesting analogy.

B: So, I am breath, and I am coming back when leaving the human shell. A moving, flowing soul is always looking to firmly connect to breath and become part of the whole or to reincarnate?

L: Let me redirect for just a second. When the "overseer" sense is successful in drawing back all the other senses, you are again complete in what we have referred to as the head of the octopus and can, if you choose, reincarnate.

B: And at that point, that portion of my soul energy is determining what it may want to learn or accumulate during a next life?

L: Yes.

B: And several "life" tentacles will be defined to learn and discover the totality of what needs to be known—the life mission, if you will?

L: You may also need to learn about things where the soul was picking up vibrations from the beginning of its existence, and that portion of your soul energy is just now becoming aware. During those moments, you might need additional tentacles to experience and learn.

B: Are you suggesting that there are "latecomers," where an octopus tentacle is dropped after all the others are reincarnated?

L: Yes, or even earlier.

B: This is where my ego begins to question all of this—that hampers my ability to grasp or understand what you are saying.

L: This goes further than you may know at this time. I use the octopus analogy only to demonstrate the connectedness of everything. Life as you now understand it is really like the Russian dolls that we have referred to in the past—it is within and within and within—including your octopus soul energy.

B: And when you say that, can I presume that my energy is always everywhere?

L: Your soul is consciousness, and it can split, shatter, and regain—it is ever flowing like the water we started with. Think of a baby for a minute. Prior to being born into human existence, it exists in fluid mostly made up of water. When it arrives, the first thing it needs to get is breath—it is the same thing for the soul.

Water and fluid are funny things. You are composed primarily of water—which is life—and you come from water. Water is a big component of this discussion, but it is not the soul and does not have the breath; think of water as one of the three major elements that make up a human shell. You need water, form, and breath to be alive.

B: Laz, it is late, and frankly, I am exhausted by this discussion; my brain hurts. Can we continue next time? But before I leave, what else do you want to bring up that would help in digesting what you have said so far?

L: What we have talked about is far from over, but to prepare for next time, I want to share with you and Shirlet the seven heavens and the seven hells.

Over this multiyear voyage, friends and family have asked many questions, but none is more frequent than this one: Who is the soul guide energy that I refer to as Laz, and what is his direct relationship with me? To answer this, I need to take a brief hiatus from the discussion on breath, with the understanding that his connection might present the proper platform to further discuss how all of this connects.

Initially, I queried everything involving this unconventional voyage—from Shirlet's talents to the subsequent presentation of spiritual newcomers or soul guides. Notwithstanding my suspicious makeup, what I was learning was completely unexpected, and by stubbornly preserving my curiosity, I quietly convinced myself to continue exploring the unusual world of souls.

While working on *Soul Sins and Regrettable Lies*, I was introduced to a principal soul guide for the first time—Laz. He was gracious, candid, perceptive, and at times both comical and upbeat with his approach to my life. To say that he was like me would not be precise—it would be more accurate to say that he looked after me, like family.

In between writing *Soul Sins and Regrettable Lies* and *Soul Mechanics: Unlocking the Human Warrior*, I was introduced to the octopus analogy and discovered that there were five souls residing within my soul's cluster group. Over the years, certain soul identities were shared, and each soul exposed a specific persona. I recognized Laz as a watcher guide, a teacher within the group. His responsibilities are centered on providing encouragement to other souls. He is the driving inspiration that occurs during moments of forewarning and unease—a protective spiritual watchdog for many lifelong mishaps. In other ways, he functions like the "overseer" that was discussed during the seven senses dialogue—by cautiously ensuring that his octopus mates are succeeding within the shifting stages of their incarnations.

My own understanding of what I have undergone with Laz—my now officially certifiable mystical experience—all remains a work in progress as I search for the right words to fully describe its outcome. It appears, however, that he serves as the maintenance department for soul-cluster energy. This is what I mean—with a subtle set of tools, he safeguards my stored energy within the head of the octopus. On occasion, along with a series of delicate prompts, he might send suggestions to benefit an outcome by way of freshly fashioned insights. Some might refer to this as an ingenious distribution of energy, allowing an earthbound soul like myself access to one's higher self.

In theory, I have no problem using the word *transcendent* to portray what I experience with both Shirlet and Laz, provided it avoids being justified in an unnerving manner. Let me clarify—uplifting personal events and information, regardless of the source, can be powerful, insightful experiences that arise when the voice of our human ego is muted or silenced.

Challenging conventional attitudes and opinions regarding how we scrutinize our existence is fertile soil for such quiet questioning. Transcendence is nothing to fear; in fact, it may be a prerequisite for making discernable spiritual progress.

Although I have not revealed this within the framework of this journey, my involvement with Laz has been sheltered to keep me from dropping behind. My spiritual life course has veered into the guardrails at times, and he has been privately covering my slipups so that I might remain with my other mates.

Having said all of this, how does my description of Laz aid in clarifying the muddled presentation of breath? First, by understanding that the connectivity to the source of spirit-world information allows for a complete spiritual context to be formed. Let me be more specific: If the fluidity of my soul energy is impeded while in the human shell, then Laz reminds me of my mobility, of who I am, from where I come, and how I was formed.

Second, by breaking from the sequence of afterlife events, he has silenced the storyline narrative, if only momentarily. In doing so, he has presented a keepsake of where my true soul family resides—within breath. His excursion along the towpath of breath has shown what my Buddhist teachers tried to tell me but I struggled to understand—that there is so much more to understand than my ego will permit to be known, and if presented to an unlocked mind, unusual possibilities can be explored.

Laz has stated that we will discuss the seven heavens and seven hells next time. I can only guess where that will lead.

CHAPTER 4

The Seven Heavens and Seven Hells

The mind is its own place, and in itself can
make a heaven of hell, a hell of heaven.
—John Milton, *Paradise Lost*

I have a Theravada Buddhist friend who taught me the internal benefits of walking meditation while we negotiated his mid-Atlantic campus in outrageous winter temperatures. He resides in a small, rustic Buddhist community several hours from my home, and on occasion, I have connected with him during my struggle to become a more sympathetic, less flawed, and slightly braver human being. Before revisiting northeastern Pennsylvania, I felt the need to reach out to him again.

Khenchen is not a physically commanding individual—he could easily get lost within a large gathering and would only be noticeable by way of his baggy, burnt-orange robe and worn sneakers. Although he is in good health and aging nicely, his diminutive, bent-over physique might leave the impression that the next strong wind could carry him away. I assure you, that is not the case.

He is an abbot for a modest group of sequestered monks and having his private contact number requires that I respect his time and seek only the moments that are available before his morning meditation. He was delighted to hear from me and agreed to have me visit the following morning just prior to morning tea—which typically occurred before five o'clock in the morning.

As I entered the front of the monastery, blurry eyed, I could see my monk friend sitting at the farthest table just outside the kitchen area. He had two small cups in front of him and a modest, decorative pot of hot water to his right. He glanced at me with a smile and pointed to the second cup with a tipped hand, mimicking a pour—I nodded my head in approval.

After we embraced, he asked if we might sit for a moment in silence—it is an exercise of discreet mindful meditation that I rarely have been able to personally master. Being acquainted with Khenchen's morning rituals from previous visits, I silently watched as he wrapped both hands around his cup, cherishing every enchanting second of his morning formality. I was envious of his concentration and calm.

Later, with his intense eyes fixed on the cup in front of him, he began to speak. Knowing that I was there to discuss the Buddhist concept of heaven and hell, he softly shared that some people need charts or directions when they find themselves lost. Once they become quiet and start to breathe softly, they begin to see their true reality: there is nowhere to go and no pathway to get there. What they seek has been with them all along. I remember him saying, "Perhaps that is what has brought you back to us today—to recognize the path that you already know."

As I sipped my tea, he pulled out a small piece of paper and stated, "I would like to read an old Buddhist story to you. Maybe it will settle this internal debate you have about heaven and hell. Can I share it with you?" I nodded, and he slowly began to read the following, pausing only to assure himself that I was attentive to the point he was making.

A tough and discourteous samurai once approached a Zen master who was in deep meditation. Impatient, the samurai demanded in his husky voice, so accustomed to forceful yelling, "Tell me the nature of heaven and hell."

The Zen master opened his eyes, looked the samurai in the face, and replied with a certain scorn, "Why should I answer to a shabby, disgusting, despondent slob like you? A worm like you, do you think I should tell you anything? I can't stand you. Get out of my sight. I have no time for silly questions."

The samurai could not bear these insults. Consumed with rage, he drew his sword and raised it to sever the master's head at once. Looking straight into the samurai's eyes, the Zen master tenderly declared, "That's hell."

The samurai froze. He immediately understood that anger had him in its grip. His mind had just created his own hell—one filled with resentment, hatred, self-defense, and fury. He realized that he was so deep in his torment that he was ready to kill somebody.

The samurai's eyes filled with tears. Setting his sword down, he put his palms together and bowed in gratitude for this insight. The Zen master gently acknowledged with a delicate smile, "And that's heaven."

As other monks began to enter the room for their morning nourishment, Khenchen talked about how his story reflected the Buddhist concepts of heaven and hell and why they were different from conventional religions. Much like the relationship between the Zen master and the samurai warrior, Buddhist lessons show that both heaven and hell are equally beyond this world and within the world we currently occupy.

Buddhists do not accept as true that the afterlife realms of delight and discomfort are never-ending. Moreover, they believe that it would be profoundly excessive to send a person to eternal hell for human fragilities. Conversely, they advocate giving individuals every chance to consistently improve themselves.

The opinion that either domain, heaven or hell, is everlasting disregards Khenchen's Eastern philosophical conviction regarding cause and effect, specifically, that the energy that governs our next human existence results from willful actions in both this life and previous incarnations. In any event, each state is impermanent, and when it is exhausted, a new life begins—a life governed by karmic energy.

I am not sure that I received the comfort I was seeking from my monk companion that morning. I am sure, however, that my expression upon returning home was one of bewilderment. Truthfully, I do not know how to better organize my thoughts for this next discussion—the proposed examination of seven heavens and seven hells.

My previous comment about taking the necessary irrevocable steps that commit me to a specific course may have been premature—perhaps that is what I am about to discover. I fear that the information about to be shared will conflict with my historical beliefs and may also be disturbingly "off the wall."

Bud: Before we start this evening, I have one question. You have used the number seven on several occasions recently; is there a reason for that?

Laz: It has the vibration to describe the act of creation. The vibration of seven, standing alone, was created out of the universe. Seven is renewal, it is challenge, and it is credibility.

Let me talk about that number and how its vibration applies to tonight's discussion. First, the seven chakras relate to both the seven heavens and the seven hells. This is how they relate. When individuals pass and go through the "tunnel," as we discussed in *Soul Mechanics: Unlocking the Human Warrior*, they are exiting with their chakra field. They are exiting with their own energy—that, in fact, is the tunnel you have always referenced. But whatever chakra level hasn't been cleansed from life's problems or challenges, that chakra holds on to the disabilities of life. The soul, therefore, connects to that energy and cannot pass through that portion of the tunnel—it is stuck at that level of the chakra, and that can become one of the seven heavens or hells we will talk about.

B: I want to make sure I understand this. If you are spinning within your energy chakra tunnel, you can essentially "stall" in one level of the chakra field and become "captured" there?

L: Yes.

B: The seven hells are the possibility that I can become stuck in one of the seven layers of the chakra upon passing?

L: Yes. Any one of the chakra levels you are passing through can be either a heaven or a hell—it depends on your vibration at the time of death. The chakra is not just spinning around you—it is a storage tank. Just as you can store life experiences in your human shell to the point of becoming ill, the same can happen to your chakra fields. You are storing your life experiences in every level of the chakra. Think, for a moment, about the spine or root level of the chakra—you would be storing sexual consistency or mating or love. You can also store what you have done to and for people in those areas.

Consider this: Within that chakra, some souls have stored how someone cheated in another loving relationship, was nasty toward a loved one, was inconsistent, or repeatedly hurt people. When this occurs, do you really think that when these people pass, they simply glide through that chakra? They cannot. They must stop at that level of the chakra to empty that chakra by themselves—they must face up to what they have done and feel the pain, the inconsistencies, or the joy of what they caused.

B: I have two questions about what you just stated. Does the soul move through each of the seven chakras simultaneously or independently?

L: Independently.

B: And you always start with the lower-level chakra—the root or spine chakra?

L: Yes.

B: How does that relate to the seven senses that we discussed several weeks ago, if at all?

L: It is very relatable. It is the senses of that chakra field that cause the disability and the storage for that soul.

B: I'm confused. We discussed the seven senses—love, hate,

peace, etcetera. Am I to understand that all seven of them operate within each chakra field and must be resolved before I can move out of the root chakra?

L: Yes.

B: OK—so I would move through the root chakra in relation to the seven senses?

L: Yes.

B: Incredible. Conversely, if I am respectful, loving, kind . . .

L: You would pass right through that level. But then you are going up to the next chakra, and that will present its own set of challenges.

B: Laz, if you could, take me through all seven of the chakra fields.

L: That would be easy. At the root level, you would be going through your relationships and how they developed—not just your sexual ones, but all your relationships with other people. That would be your root chakra; we refer to it as your earth chakra—the chakra you have on this planet. It represents your grounding choice of whether you wanted to have relationships or chose to be close to somebody—how you treated others when you were with them.

B: I assume it is important to resolve any karma any of us have at this level—if not, we could be trapped within that chakra until we find a way to resolve it within ourselves, correct?

L: For anyone—absolutely.

B: Seems to me that this process might be a way of explaining the "life review" in a more sophisticated manner. Can I look at it that way?

L: Yes and no. Let me move on further. The next is your sixth level; I call it the children or life chakra. Here you review questions like how you treated your children, if any, and how you treated all creation. How did you treat any-thing that was created? How did you treat animals, people, life? Overall, have you been decent with creation, or did you just live your life carelessly, harming creation? Did you get what creation was all about intentionally and, as a result, breeze right through this level? Or did you do something horrendously evil—such as painfully torturing animals or people, especially children? If so, you would be there for some time.

B: You are using different names to describe the chakras.

Shirlet: Yes, he is. What I find interesting, however, is that the one he just talked about is where the womb is located, and it makes sense that he would see it as creation.

L: Now, the next chakra is the chakra of your belief system—the solar plexus. I see it as the chakra of God, it is the chakra of "all-knowing." The chakra of connections, of life, of the life-giving energies of water and light, of everything around you that makes you human.

B: You are referring to a higher-level review of life, correct?

L: Yes. You would not want to get stuck in this chakra and have a review. Understanding who you have been in life and who you truly are moves you quickly through this level.

The next would be your heart chakra—your fourth level. This chakra has many complications because it is all about love—it is at the heart. What did you do with the love that was experienced? What did you do with the love you could have given? Did you miss giving love? Did you take opportunities where you could have given love and instead gave hate, deception, or lies? What did you do with the love that was presented in your life—did you realize it, acknowledge it, nurture it? This is a higher chakra.

B: What would happen if love was ignored?

L: It would be no different. You would see it for what it was—that you isolated it and fell away from love, from caring, from sharing. Missing the love of a mate, the love of an animal, the love of a child, the love of a friend. That would be a lonely review—would it not?

The next chakra is all about what you say, the thorax. It is a chakra of power because words have power. Words can destroy life or give life. A word can build a city, and one word can level one. During your life, what did your words do to people? How did you leave them feeling when you walked away from them? This is the chakra of what your words did. Did they sting or bite like a snake? Did they destroy people and make them sad, cause them to cry, or make them afraid of you? Or did your words calm them and show them love and caring, conveying that you were there for them? Did your words show them that they meant something in your life?

B: I have questions, but I want to wait until you are finished.

L: The next to discuss is your awareness chakra—the center forehead. It contains your storage, the Akashic records of who you truly were and what is truly going on around you. It contains your ability to see through the obvious. This chakra is also what you will do about the things that you see. For example, if you see destruction, are you trying to do something about it? Have you used this chakra to save life, or have you let life die? This is the knowledge of an all-knowing chakra.

Finally, the top chakra, which is in your crown—there is a reason for its position—is your soul's exit point. Not only that, the crown represents your total knowledge—it is your mind, it is everything that you have learned. Consider yourself a computer system: What have you learned from others?

What have you taught or shown them? Have you made a difference in their lives? Have you made them want to live, want to thrive, and want to be the best that they can be? What did you do with this chakra before you exited?

B: I have a question about all seven of the chakra fields. I am examining or reviewing my life successes or failures as I move through the chakra levels as a soul—correct?

L: Yes. It is as if it is happening to you all over again.

B: And the intention is for me to experience what I have done so that I can take corrective action going forward?

L: Yes. Once you exit the human shell, you will have an awareness of all the chakra issues sticking to you, and each of these chakra issues has changed your energy field. And your energy-field vibration determines whether you go into the heaven or hell side of each chakra.

There are two types of heavens and hells, one set that plays out within the chakras and one that can occur within human terms.

B: Will we talk about both?

L: Perhaps.

S: I think he is suggesting that as you move through the

chakras, the materials you have picked up, whether determined to be a representation of heaven or hell, affect your frequency both in the spirit world and here on this planet.

B: Laz, is it possible that the overall experience is a cleansing process?

L: Unfortunately, both yes and no. It can be a cleansing or the opposite, where it could bring the soul down and become problematic.

B: Because of guilt?

L: Absolutely. If, for example, a man murdered twenty people, he would not come away from this review feeling positive about his advancement. That pain is stuck on him.

B: Does that type of pain get resolved through a new incarnation, or is there something that can be done for a soul to relieve this?

L: No. There would not be a quick incarnation. There would, however, be an evaluation period. If such souls led a decent life and had this type of pain on them, a small portion of their energy is still living through this pain here on this planet—it is one of the hells. This portion of their energy stays on this planet and might help others or try to correct what had occurred. Finally, when they reincarnate, that is when they will have to completely digest and account for what they have done in the previous life—that is what judgment is all about.

B: I don't want to get lost in any of this: If that individual soul moves through the seven chakras in alignment with the seven senses, the weight of its actions remain on the soul until the soul is ready to incarnate again? And for that soul to carry the weight of past actions, is that like another soul hell?

L: Yes.

B: To balance this out, what would be an example of a soul heaven?

L: The opposite of that would be for the soul to be able to move quickly through the chakras, feeling as though it has done something extraordinary for the human world and its people. That it made a difference and is now set at a higher vibration level and might even decide not to reincarnate again but to watch over others.

B: Like a graduation?

L: Yes. Being able to ascend beyond incarnations is the best.

B: Laz, would you be an example of that?

L: Been there, done that.

B: I want to clean up one aspect of this. Is it possible that a soul who had a negative life on this planet and, as a result, experiences a type of soul hell in spirit could be given another chance, in a human shell, to make amends?

L: Yes. It is not with a soul's free will, however. Souls may be given another opportunity to work things out, but only if they fully realize what they have done. Ironically, souls in that position can haunt a home or an area for a lifetime and remain in that state until they are ready to reincarnate.

B: Souls that are on that side of the chakra review, the hell side, they can be haunting on their planet of origin?

L: Yes, within the life they led.

B: Essentially, does that explain why some people think they experience malevolent spirits? Would such a spirit represent a soul that passed, experienced the process of the seven chakras and seven senses, and ended up back on this planet?

S: In essence, as I interpret this, Bud, they know what they did and are temporarily immobilized or lack the ability to advance spiritually until they completely understand what they did.

B: Is it the same as a soul that moved through a chakra level and is stuck with the sense of hate? You shared earlier that hate is a very powerful sense and often results in a haunting.

L: I did. Not every soul is remorseful about a life experience. Many times, they represent younger, developing souls with limited human lives.

B: I imagine that as a soul moves through each of the chakra fields, both heavens and hells, the weighing scales are raised and lowered depending on the "review" that the soul is receiving—is that a way of understanding all of this?

S: That is exactly what he is saying—incredible.

B: This might not be the most appropriate question, but can souls witness another soul's review? And if so, how do they look upon that?

L: Yes, but they often withdraw or distance themselves from another's chakra hell.

B: I assume that there are spiritual resources that can be made available to a soul in that position.

L: Yes. A soul guide would orchestrate that type of intervention or resource.

B: Would that include any of the soulmates that are residing in the head of that soul's octopus?

L: Yes. They can help—there is a "get out of jail" card—but not a lot of them are made available. They get used only if the soul has done some good during its incarnation.

One thing to think about is that if there has been a serious event, like a murder that was committed, that soul could be "grounded" for a long time, and it would require additional souls to intervene. These souls can be stuck in chakra loops, where they are continuously experiencing the murder events over and over.

B: You told me previously that souls who experience a life-trauma event get trapped in that event. Are you suggesting that those souls get caught in a chakra loop? And could that portion of the soul's energy be trapped on earth?

L: Yes.

B: Surely there are spiritual resources available to those souls to break the loop?

L: Yes. What is important is for the soul to recognize and accept that type of assistance.

B: Hypothetically, if I made some serious errors in life, and the soulmates within the head of my octopus could not shake me out of a chakra loop, is there a higher level to appeal to?

L: Again, the answer would be yes. It would be a creator.

Something to think about before we conclude is that it is important to consider what chakras need to be cleansed now rather than waiting and discovering those issues after you pass. Imagine what you might experience if you landed on the heaven side of each chakra review—what wonderful energies you would encounter.

B: Laz, what is for next time?

L: The effect that "thought-forms" have on the afterlife.

From this dialogue, my initial afterlife question takes center stage—specifically, what happens when I stop breathing and completely detach from my body?

Clearly, Laz suggested that how I put together my after-life puzzle depends on who I think I am and what life skir-mishes I selected while alive. For example, if I think I am just this body and mind—just my memories and experiences, relationships, and thoughts—then death is sure to be very bad news. His reasoning behind that? Because when I die, I will lose my ego's protection against past human exploits and con-front what Khenchen called my "true reality." Once there, the resolution of my life's actions is not only necessary, but it is required.

With everything that has been revealed, I have this question: If I am meticulous and effective with this trial, is a fast-paced resolution of my karma events likely?

Here is the suggestion Laz has given to answer that question: If I adjust my energy vibration before death, I can square off in settlement with every specified action and thought that was carried out in my life. However, if left unattended, these acts can represent a frightening, long-term, weighty life review within each chakra level.

I need to come clean for a moment. This afterlife expedition has resulted in some uneasy debates—the octopus-head phenomenon of soul division, exposure to multiple afterlife senses, and now a tailspin journey of karma attachments to my energy field. If all of this is true, then it should be no surprise that disorientation and uncertainty are the likely primary impressions for an unsuspecting soul upon passing.

I have two private thoughts on what has been shared so far. First, perhaps the act of soul splitting is intentionally designed. Here is my logic for saying this: With the assortment of chaotic activity inflicted at the point of passing, it is conceivable that the process of soul fragmenting affords my soul energy the opportunity to better navigate what is being witnessed. Remaining a singular source of energy may only serve to heighten a soul's confusion and stoke unnecessary fear. If so, faceting would make sense.

Second, the release of soul energy into the seven layers of chakras and seven senses may simply be a by-product of an impending dam release. If the human shell is a containment vessel of soul energy, is it possible that energy separation is a natural occurrence and not as abnormal as it seems at first?

I still have one remaining and persistent question for Laz at this point: At any time, are the ego energy and consciousness of Bud Megargee traveling independently through the layers of an afterlife, to join later with the other faceted energy particles within the head of the octopus? If not, I fear I am in trouble.

Next up—thought-form energies and how they add to this puzzle.

CHAPTER 5

What Thoughts Create

On occasion, when I close my eyes, random thoughts seem to fashion images that spring forth as if the inside of my lids were showing a feature film. This makes me wonder: Are these visions basically life projections formed by thoughts that are captured within a moment of time and boxed into a picture show?

Considering everything that has been said up to this point, I honestly do not know what to make of this experience. Within this journey of all journeys, I am convinced that I need to be fully prepared for a total mental reboot—one that requires a temporary disabling of my ego in order to fully understand the actuality of a soul afterlife.

These past months, I have repeatedly asked myself, What have I learned during this unrestricted period of soul-afterlife investigation? As I wrote this question in my notebook, I felt that it represented a straightforward problem, yet my solutions were colored by the use of spiritual surrogates to find my answers, which, by any standard, is anything but routine or straightforward.

To separate out any ongoing confusion, I am left with this arresting position: that the subjective assimilation of all that has been shared has been intentionally cursory. My conclusion? That Laz might be calling for me to burrow out from under all these teachings as if they were my own—essentially, that I need to find my own path to unanswered questions.

Here are my primary observations prior to my next visit to discuss thought-forms: Often, my thoughts go around and around as if they are trapped within a loop of foolishness. Most of these ideas do not fall on the side of being useful—some distract from quiet moments with the intent to create mental mayhem. During those instants, I have convinced myself that I am not causing any harm by simply thinking of something, but the reality is that the thoughts that occupy real estate in my brain are slowly being jettisoned into the universe, and I have no idea where they will settle.

My Buddhist friends refer to thinking as "noble silence"—indicating that thoughts are like a candle that radiates light, heat, and scent. Similarly, thinking manifests itself in various ways—some I will be on familiar terms with, whereas others will remain mysterious.

I tend to hold tightly to my thoughts. This may seem strange to some, but I believe that they are a real part of who I am, and to let go might just give up part of who I am becoming.

With the initiation of thought-forms, I need to resolve this issue: What is about to be revealed to me? Surely, the topic of thought-forms is just an additional hallway filled with infinity mirrors, posing thoughtful challenges in understanding the complexity of a soul's afterlife. I am counting on that being the case.

Bud: Laz, I have a question: When thoughts are attached to a human emotion, is that when they become beliefs?

Laz: You are both right and wrong with that question. Thoughts have always been thoughts, since creation. Everything you can think of has already been done; it has been in the universe—when you think of it, then it is drawn toward you.

B: Are thoughts like little energy packets or bubbles of energy that are looking for a resonance to affix to?

L: Think of a lizard sitting on a branch and extending its tongue to capture an insect—that is what it's like with a thought. Think, for a moment, of all the facets of your soul and all the thoughts from those facets becoming solid for just your shell.

B: Are you suggesting to me that there are no original thoughts?

L: At this point in time, maybe very few are original. With all the thoughts from people existing over millions of years, what would you think?

B: Could I use the thunderstorm analogy that you explained

previously to understand what you have just said? Am I walking through wave after wave of thoughts, where each raindrop represents a historical thought floating in the universe?

L: Absolutely. Here is another example. Assume that you want a new car, as have many others. That thought is hanging out there, just a step away from you. Think of your thought reaching out and grabbing hold of that thought and pulling it into you. Imagine the concentration, energy, and focus it would take for you to differentiate it from other thoughts. That is how thoughts are created in solid form.

B: Because thought is a form of my energy?

L: That brings you to a question before we talk about how this affects the afterlife: how you create thought-forms while you are living in a human shell.

B: Describe that in more detail.

L: Imagine that you are in front of ten caves, and whatever cave you choose, you will experience what you have thought is in that cave. People who use their energy worrying or obsessing about things create what they have thought.

B: Are those thoughts already in existence, as you have suggested?

L: Yes. It is like when someone goes fishing. You throw a line into your powerful mind, and you get what you hook, what your mind truly wants.

B: Let's make a transition to the afterlife of a soul and the impact of thoughts. How does this relate to the seven heavens, seven hells, and seven senses?

L: If you have applied enough energy to something, you will have created it, including all the associated emotions. Here is an example. If you had bullied someone while playing when you were younger, upon passing, you will revisit that event and that playground. It will be reenacted, but you will be the one feeling all the punches as well as everything that the one you were bullying was thinking, punch after punch.

B: At that time, am I experiencing all the thoughts that I had in those moments?

L: Actually, no. You would see them and feel them—it is more that you are experiencing how others thought about you. You experience how you have left people.

B: Are these the thoughts that have the capacity to take form?

L: Yes, when you are out of the human shell. When you are in the human shell, you can create solid form from your thoughts. Do you understand the difference?

B: Yes, that explains the bullying example.

L: You can also experience the opposite. Say that you stopped by the bus depot and comforted a woman who was having a bad day. You would have experienced gratitude and love from that individual for having taken the time to help. The same for someone who saved an animal from the cold—that soul would feel the thoughts of that animal's love.

B: Laz, I am imagining a tidal wave of experiences that the soul faces while it is navigating its afterlife path.

L: It will go through what it believed in. For example, if someone believed in Buddha, then that person would be with Buddha. If people believed that they would be going to hell, then that is what they would initially experience. If they believed they would be going into heaven, where they would be walking with Jesus and God, then that is what they would experience. After that, they would begin counting down through all these thought-forms and how they made others feel.

B: I need to understand what you just said: Whatever afterlife experience I believed in, that is what I will initially experience before I enter a "life review" with the seven heavens and seven hells?

L: Yes, because you created it. It is a primary afterlife memory.

B: I realize that time is not an issue in the afterlife, but can you give me an example of how long that initial experience would last?

L: Seconds, but you would think it is much longer.

B: After that initial experience, does the soul feel confused by all the chaos of the seven layers?

L: It is more a feeling of remorse and gratitude. If you were a good person, there would be extreme gratitude toward the creator and your creations. You would move through the layers quickly, see loved ones, and so forth. You would go through all the steps I described. The biggest outcome is that you must feel what others thought and all their pain and love. To put it bluntly, what you have done is done to you.

B: What is unique to tonight's discussion is the introduction of the thoughts that I have had and the thoughts about me from others and how they play out in the afterlife.

L: That is right—you will know every thought you had, and the thoughts others have had toward you.

B: Laz, I must be honest with you here—that may be more terrifying because it is a hidden expectation of a life review. I think most would understand that we would have account-ability for the actions we took, but not our thoughts.

L: It illustrates how powerful the human mind really is—does it not?

B: I have an odd thought: When another soul has its review, do I participate in that review if I have had thoughts toward that soul?

L: Yes.

B: Regardless of whether I have reincarnated?

L: Yes.

B: A faceted portion of my energy that is still in spirit would be a participant in all of that?

L: Yes.

B: I am taken aback by the complexity of all of this. I guess that if you have thought about something, you probably should have just acted on it, because the accountability is the same.

L: It goes to the pinpoint of life. Think, for a moment, about a spider on the floor that you are about to step on—you will experience the pain it will feel and the thought it has at that second.

B: With thoughts like this, what can I do before I pass to balance all of this?

L: It is what you just said; it is balance. For every tear you contributed toward, you must make someone laugh. It does not have to be the same person, but for everyone you made sad, you must balance that with comfort, love, and belonging.

B: Especially regarding how I have thought about things or people?

L: If there is no balance, then there is the serious risk of being caught in one of the seven heavens or seven hells and becoming trapped until it is all resolved—or, as you have said, is balanced.

B: Without an understanding of the impact of thoughts, I can see any one of us getting self-trapped in one of the seven senses or even one of the seven heavens or seven hells simply out of ignorance.

L: That is easily resolved. Read the book [the Bible]—Jesus said that to have thought it, is to have done it. Wouldn't it make sense to raise your vibration and do your life review now and not have the fear of being trapped?

B: This is a lot to digest.

L: You have to ascend and raise your energy field. Here is the best way to understand and avoid this trap: Imagine that every time you have a negative thought, I hand you a brick.

Every time you do something where you upset somebody, hurt somebody, I give you a brick. Think now—how many bricks would you hold if you were to pass? If you have those bricks, you cannot ascend to a vibration level that you might call a heaven.

Imagine again that you are holding twenty bricks, and they are getting heavy. There is a lady having trouble with her bags as she leaves a store, and you help her; I take a brick away. If you have lied in the past but now you are truthful to everyone you meet, I take another brick away. If you think in these terms, you can understand how to correct negative thought-forms.

B: I like this analogy.

L: Take this advice: try to eliminate as many bricks as you can before you pass; otherwise, they just might turn into a giant unmovable wall.

B: Awareness of the accumulation of bricks is not enough?

L: Balance and self-awareness are critical—if you hate yourself, you just gave yourself a brick. If you put yourself down, you have given yourself a brick. It is not just others who can throw bricks at you.

B: Is it also possible that if you have harmed someone in the past, you are not only carrying that brick but adding bricks as time passes because you have not balanced that out?

L: One hundred percent. It is mostly the absence of self-compassion, but also the absence of forgiving others, forgiving yourself, and moving on. Also, good people who experienced something from a distance but did nothing to change it put themselves at risk of accumulating unwanted bricks. They blame themselves, and in doing so, they give themselves another brick.

B: That is sad, because it may not be warranted or deserved.

L: Absolutely. When that happens, it places a blemish on part of your soul's energy field. What is important is this: What do people do with what has happened to them? For example, if they turn a distant bad event into a positive response, they will remove accumulated bricks—it is all how you deal with it.

B: Bricks are actions or thoughts?

L: Exactly. Too many bricks can cause some people to become ill—that is why associating with negative people is not good for your health.

B: Laz, before we end tonight, I want to bring up something that you promised we would discuss. At the very end of *Soul Imprints: The Legacy of Existence*, you asked me to list four things that I wished to accomplish before I passed. You then asked that I save talking about them until we discussed the creation of thought-forms. Can you share your goal for this exercise with me now? My four desired accomplishments before passing are (1) unquestionable confidence, (2) increased emotional vulnerability, (3) finishing everything that has been started, and (4) removing as much negative karma as possible.

My question today is this: How do these four goals relate to what we have discussed about thoughts and the afterlife?

Laz: We can do that now if you like. Let's go over them one at a time.

B: OK. Start with unquestionable confidence.

L: That can be part of your personal control issues. Your confidence would come from understanding that you cannot control people and how they respond to you. You can, however, control how you receive what others are saying about you and what you do with all of that.

B: Shifting the control from the outside to the inside—by controlling myself? But how does that assist me in the afterlife?

L: You would have controlled the creation of thought-forms and not have as many bricks as you have now. From my position, it is very simple. What is the next one on your list?

B: Becoming more emotionally vulnerable in this life.

L: This would help with your control issues as well, but there is a limit to becoming emotionally vulnerable. If you are too emotionally vulnerable, then you will automatically accept other people's bricks. Their actions will upset you enough that you will accumulate the bricks—so there is a fine line here. Rather than accepting emotional vulnerability, it would be wise to look at it as becoming emotionally available. By becoming compassionate toward yourself, you are in touch with your true feelings without accepting other people's baggage or bricks.

B: What about my desire to complete everything that I start?

L: There is no reason why anyone should not complete what they wish. In your situation, one stumbling block or giant mountain to climb is how you worry so much about other people's opinions. When you shed what they think of you, what you do, and how you do it, you will accomplish everything that you started in life. If you continue to rely on others' thought patterns, then all you are doing is exchanging bricks back and forth and getting nowhere.

B: Lastly, working to remove as much negative karma as possible.

L: In part, you are already doing some of that by undertaking this voyage. The justification for yourself, the annunciation of who you truly are and your position within your soul, has always been about removing negative karma. You do all of this with tools and information because the knowledge you gain over time is power, and that helps to get the negative karma out of your life. The biggest obstacle that you currently have is controlling your emotions. Do not choose detrimental emotions, because they only result in the weight of additional bricks.

B: Is there anything more to add?

L: What you are asking for, you can accomplish. Your four thoughts are not extreme and could easily be brought into a positive thought-form. The biggest dragon on your back will always be your emotions and how you respond to situations. You still have time to remove all of your unwanted bricks.

B: Laz, next time, in what direction will we take our afterlife discussion?

L: It is time to talk about reincarnation—that would be the next step after a soul returns to the octopus head, fully charged with its energy. This will be a wide-ranging topic.

I am a fan of the Starbucks Corporation business plan, and it has very little to do with the company's pick-me-up drink selection. It is my belief that Starbucks has positioned itself as the modern-day version of an Irish pub or the replacement for the old Wild West saloons. At any given moment, almost anything goes within a Starbucks's four walls.

Sumatra coffee and frosty Frappuccino's are not within my daily beverage budget, but I do use Starbucks's facilities to attest to some of the challenges I am exposed to during this journey. As a recent example, while working through the challenges of thought-forms, I did the following: One morning while standing in line, I turned to the man behind me and asked if he had any idea as to where thoughts came from. I watched as a frown formed on this elderly gentleman's face while he slowly shifted his body position farther away from me. He was secretly struggling to understand the question and the reason I asked it in the first place; I received no answer. Later, as I approached the counter, I posed this idea to my cashier—I asked if she was aware that neurosurgeons have yet to find a human thought upon opening the skull during any present-day craniotomy procedure. She just looked intently at me for a moment, then sought out my change without saying a word—I fear I may have given her an unwanted brick.

My findings from these somewhat bizarre coffee bar adventures? We are indeed observers of the world that our mind creates, due to the method by which we form and project our thoughts toward ourselves and those around us.

With wide-ranging thought activities available every second of the day, I have the capacity to generate remarkable change and break from conventional patterns to open up new possibilities—and the driver behind this is the way I observe myself, everyone I encounter, and the unseen world of thought that envelops me.

Quantum physics states that something can come into existence only when it is observed. That means something exists because my mind first thought it into existence—scientifically, this is known as quantum potentiality. Perhaps this is the scientific answer for what Laz has suggested with his explanation of how I can create thought-forms while in a human shell.

My biggest takeaway from this discussion is that every thought, even the most insignificant, is a living reality. Michael Dooley, one of the presenters in the movie *The Secret*, fittingly suggested that if I want to know what my thoughts look like, I should just look around wherever I stand—keeping in mind this phrase: thoughts are created into things.

Everything I perceive in the physical world has its origin in the invisible—my innermost world of thoughts and beliefs. Laz submits that this thought power is the explanation of my current reality, and the reconciliation of those events is guaranteed upon my passing.

My learning from this discussion? To develop a passageway with a vibration for my soul's growth, I need to consciously balance out my interior thought domain and construct healthy resolutions to any suffering, or bricks, that I may have consciously or mistakenly created.

Next: examining the process of soul reincarnation.

CHAPTER 6

Soul Reincarnation

At a certain time in life, most of us stop questioning the remarkable experience of our everyday surroundings. For example, we might savor the beauty of a crystal-clear blue sky, but for some reason, we no longer question how it arrived at that color. What happened to the carefree human impulses that allow us to explore the answers to creation?

It is not enough to logically know about a soul's afterlife or the intended act of spiritual reincarnation. I need to rationally understand how my energy fits into such a progression. My thinking is this: If I could graph this process, I might be able to provide myself with an empowering talent that would consistently fuel my unshakable curiosity. It would not be some magical gift bestowed by unfamiliarity, but a product of my return to a view of childlike innocence—an outlook designed to figure out why there are things that I cannot fully understand.

I am learning that becoming relentlessly curious about the life of a soul requires taking small, unwavering steps. It is like reading a newly purchased five-hundred-page book—it cannot be dusted off with a simple human stare. My desire to seek spiritual knowledge for its own sake is a worthy task, but I suspect it needs to be woven together in unity with the purpose of this journey; otherwise, why would I board such a train and voluntarily depart the station?

I have always trusted that the complexion of all life is cyclical. For example, without exception, daylight fades to dusk, then shifts into complete darkness, only to return to daylight when the sun rises.

As a result, I throw away the calendars that my real estate agent sends to me at the beginning of each new year—why bother? I inherently know that each seasonal phase gives way to the next; it's always clear-cut and flawless. Students who study the lineage charts of descendants, as well as the consumers of Ancestry.com products, continuously observe that new generations are born, and long-established ones pass away. What is surprising, however, is that despite the ongoing cycle of birth, death, and rebirth that saturates nature, many belief systems still defend that human existence is exclusively linear.

I find it interesting that ancient observers looked at the progression of human existence and decided that, like the natural world, life might actually be more cyclical than linear. Conceivably, their debates regarding the carrying over of life might begin to explain why some religions, philosophies, and movements are slowly adopting a belief in the cycle of life and the possibility of a reawakening soul.

I assume that Laz will pilot his own course on the subject of reincarnation. As for me, I am questioning how the process of soul continuation transpires—the details that would follow a very complex life review. As always, I am interested in what he may say.

Laz: Let's see how you will understand reincarnation. I would like you to hold out your hand, and in its palm, place a very dangerous bee—one that has a poison stinger. I would like you to swat it.

Bud: OK—done.

L: Now, what have you just done?

B: I just murdered a bee.

L: Think spiritually. What have you just done to that bee?

B: Have I released its energy?

L: In a way, yes. You have taken away its shell. So, where did the energy go? Did it die?

B: No—because energy cannot die.

L: Correct. So again, where did it go?

B: I guess it went to where all insect energy travels.

L: Somewhat—but what I was looking for is that it went to the consciousness memories of the bee. Energy has a memory, and these memories come from the shell. When you lose your shell, you still can go through your memories—that is why when people pass, they see their lives flash before them within the levels we discussed before. They are actually reviewing and experiencing all of their memories.

B: And these memories are projected within the soul's seven senses and aura?

L: Yes. Now with all of this in mind, the memories this bee had when it was living will come together in one climax of life. These memories will tell the bee one thing, and it will have a code. What do you think that code tells the bee energy?

B: Does it represent the bee's potential incarnation going forward?

L: Yes. It will tell the bee energy that it was a bee and that it can reincarnate as a bee again.

B: Will that energy always be restricted to just becoming an insect?

L: It could elevate, but if all the memories were telling it within its code that it was an insect, then it will likely become an insect again.

B: Is it the same if human memories project that a soul will be going to heaven—then they would go to that memory upon passing?

L: Consider this for a moment: Think of all the different people who die on your planet each day. As we discussed last time, some see Jesus, some Buddha, some other things. What does that tell you?

B: I assume they were the human memories present at the time of passing.

L: Yes. So, when you are thinking about reincarnation, you are running a ridge of memories. The mind is very powerful, Bud. I am not talking about the human brain, but the subconscious mind—your transcendent mind. This mind was reincarnated from the very beginning; it runs throughout all time, every place, and all sound. Reincarnation has everything to do with the memories because it is your memories that pull the mind in the correct direction after death.

Assume for a minute that you are standing in the middle of ten freeways; they all go in a different direction, and you have to pick which one to travel. But there is only one that has something for you. How do you choose it? This is the reason that memories are vital to reincarnation—they are the signposts that point you in the proper direction. It is almost like a book that you are reading, and then you get to write the next chapter.

B: Is this sequential in its makeup? What I mean is this: If in a past life I was a laboring seaman on a merchant vessel, could I progress forward and reincarnate as the first mate or captain next time?

L: That could be correct, but you also could reincarnate in the other direction and be the one who walks the plank.

B: What determines the movement up or down that reincarnation ladder?

L: Very simply, it is sound and its vibration. Everything is connected in the universe by sound. The sound of breath—we talked about this previously. The sound of being, the sound and vibration that you make with a single thought. Your reincarnation rests on your memories but also on sound. Sound is the most important thing, because without sound, you would not be able to incarnate.

B: So, you are suggesting that the different vibrations of sound determine what happens within the next incarnation?

L: Yes.

B: I assume, then, that it is not as simple as having a desire to become, say, a concert pianist in Europe?

L: Sadly, no, unless you started down that road now by

working toward it with concentration and energy, so that your sound and memories were compatible with the desire—then you would have something. There has to be a firm and solid connection to your desire.

B: Is it like developing a reincarnation blueprint prior to passing?

L: In a way, yes. But do not minimize the necessity of having a connection to all of this. As an example, where in Europe, and have you visited there with your energy? Is a piano in your life now, and is it somehow connected to your energy? Or is all of this just thought or human desire?

B: Is the driver behind one's next incarnation what is to be learned?

L: What is interesting about what you learn and when you learn it is that time is not a barrier—plus, reincarnation can put you anywhere within time. It could put you in 1913, or in 1000 BC, or 350 AD, or it could put you on different planet or within a different universe—there are no barriers to your learning.

B: If I had no understanding of what you have shared, could the development or design of my future incarnations become chaotic or haphazard?

L: You might be right. Typically, in situations like that, the incarnations are stalled out. A person would be in the same area, with the same families and associates, involving the same life challenges and situations.

B: Could I look at it like a rebooting of the same life cycle?

L: Yes. If you did not have what we have talked about prior to passing, you would not be in a position to change the life cycle you have referenced.

B: Let's stop for a moment so that I can gather my thoughts, because this is unlike anything I have imagined or have read about.

There are some who believe that there are occasions in the afterlife when souls are given the opportunity to simply select and then review anticipated incarnations. They would review them on a screen and actually be able to test-drive what those lives would be like. Is that similar to your point of view?

L: Hardly. In an instance like what you describe, they are simply exploring their memories—there is no projection room here.

B: These memories display a historical reality, correct?

L: Let me take this a step further. You have seen this before when a person dies; the doctor revives the body, and upon waking, the person can now speak a foreign language or play a piano symphony. Ironically, the soul has already reincarnated, and what is awakening is the past memories of that soul.

B: Are you suggesting that the current version of that soul's energy is not coming back?

L: Correct, it is not coming back—it is the reincarnated energy of that soul.

B: Again, I need to stop and review all of this so that I do not get lost. As a soul passes through the afterlife progression you have previously described and returns to the octopus head, that soul is now loaded with the memories of all the appendage incarnations that were dropped. Does that soul have access to the memories from all of those appendages, and do they play a role in the next incarnation? Could that be the reason that a new talent is brought out?

L: Yes, but your energy—that energy you identify as Bud Megargee—does not need those other memories; you will have your own.

B: So, I have passed, and all this energy is available to me, but my new incarnations are based solely upon my Bud Megargee memories, despite the availability of other energy?

L: Correct—the ego you are concerned about is no longer

involved. That is a human problem, not a spiritual one, that affects future incarnations.

B: That is different from my understanding. To simplify all of this, take a moment and review for me what happens when souls pass.

L: Usually, they see the body, they see how they died, and they hear everything that is going on. All things become very powerful. The sound is like nothing they have heard before because the shell is no longer hindering them. Their vibration level of energy is at its highest achieved power and is not being drained by the human shell. The soul is out, and it is free. With that comes incredible perception. For example, they see colors like they have never imagined. They know what is going on, and they can be anywhere with the speed of a thought. They know what anybody ever said or thought instantly—good and bad. They know what is going to happen—they know the future. They have instant knowledge of the world they have departed.

B: If they know the future, do they also know what will happen with a possible new incarnation?

L: No, it is the future of the planet they have departed that is now part of the soul's awareness.

B: How does knowing that affect their decisions regarding a new incarnation?

L: It is a possible hindrance, because if they see a friend or family member in trouble, they may try to incarnate too soon or, in other cases, wait too long.

B: I would like you to explain the importance of having a connection to any new incarnation, because I would assume that a past connection like you just referenced might be a problem.

L: I would like you to do something for me. I would like you to sit up and pretend that you are going fishing. I would like you to throw out your line and see it go into the water. Now I want you to try to reel in a fish and realize that, suddenly, you have no string on the fishing rod. How can you possibly pull in a fish?

B: I get it—no connection. I can throw any thought or possible reincarnation request into the universe, but without some solid connection, it is like fishing without a line—and the same would be with past loved ones.

L: That is, it.

B: Is it magical, in a way, this process of reincarnation?

L: Why would it not be? But there are some higher, more advanced souls that get involved so that an incarnation selection remains appropriate and avoids becoming too carefree and/or manipulative.

B: Is that to ensure that there are meaningful learnings taking place, regardless of what connected fishing lines I am throwing out?

L: Absolutely.

B: Do these advanced souls act as reviewers, and are they part of a soul's council? I have read that every soul presents to a council of elders.

L: Yes, but I am not sure they would like the term *elder*. They want to see that a soul works for learning and advancement. If someone truly does not want to work for something, why should that person have it? What could you learn from a situation like that? It is all about desire and thought. If you cannot create the thought, and you cannot create where it would fall, then you fail.

B: Does a soul have to present its newly thought-out and connected incarnation to the council before proceeding?

L: Not always, but you would have discussed the plan with your "mates" back in the head of the octopus; they would know before you go and present something to your council— after all, you are all part of the same energy.

One thing we have not talked about and I need to introduce here is that there is a double of every soul energy—that affects a soul's learning. All souls have a double within them—it is the opposite of what they are; it mirrors them and is one breath away from them on an energy plane of existence.

B: What is the purpose of a soul having an opposite? Is it the yin and yang of a learning experience?

L: It has to be that way; it is the method of learning all that is to be learned—the good and the bad.

B: Can I assume that every version of a soul's energy, including all the "appendages," has a double version of that incarnation experience?

L: Yes. The challenge is that the opposite needs to learn through you, and you have to learn for it as well—I find that interesting.

B: Exactly how does this learning get transferred or translated?

L: It is transferred both mentally and emotionally, but typically, a soul never knows where it is coming from. For example, you might experience some unfounded fear, and that may be coming from the double who is completely unlike you. On the other hand, your learning could creep into the double's existence—in either case, that soul chooses to take in what is being transferred.

B: Does that answer why some of us have odd instincts?

L: Not really, because what we are talking about comes in the form of an energy burst, not an instinct.

B: Could that be an unusual feeling that overtakes me?

L: Yes, but again, it is not coming from you. If you are feeling inadequate or like nothing is working, you are experiencing what the double is feeling, and it has zapped you. Here is a way to understand this—think of both of you standing back to back, and from time to time, you are passing energy back and forth. In some circles, people refer to them as spiritual doppelgangers.

B: So, to shed some light on this, all reincarnation plans are implemented with a double, but that double could be in another dimension or somewhere else?

L: Yes, because the path of learning requires that a soul learn all it can, good and bad; you can't learn one without the other, or there would be no existence.

B: Understanding that all souls meet or review their plans with a council prior to an incarnation, can you describe a typical session with these higher souls?

L: You go in and meet with all thirteen and sit at what you would call a half-moon table. The members are from all different origins, some of which you would not recognize. They are all incredibly powerful. As soon as you enter, you are informed as to why you are there. Then you present your-self or your incarnation arguments to them, and they give you their feedback and what could happen—it is all very clear.

B: With free will, I can choose to take their recommendations or not?

L: They do not much care because their word is done, and you live with the consequences of your decisions.

B: Can you explain who these souls are—could they be original souls?

L: Maybe you could describe them that way. They are the same grand council members for every soul, including me. You might also like to know that in addition to the council members, each soul has two good primary guides and two that are not so good to give input during an incarnation—again, the yin and yang of existence.

B: Laz, with all of this input and review, how does reincarnation actually take place?

L: What do you mean? It just does.

B: As an example, if I am reincarnating on this planet, how would my soul pick which family it will be born into or which parent to choose?

L: You would pick them; you always have that option. As a soul, you have a lot of energy and power, and you have lifetimes of accomplishments. If you did positive things during your past lives, you would simply choose your next environment/situation.

From a practical point of view, you are literally looking through different dimensions for all the possibilities. It would be analogous to watching a giant television of a future parent's life. Additionally, if you want to, you could go there in spirit and hang around them for a time until you decide to incarnate. But this does not always happen—sometimes if a soul's energy is low, and the soul just casually reincarnates, that soul may acquire people who are not helpful as parents; it is a dicey proposition and a bad situation. In a case like this, the soul has not had a choice in the selection because its energy is extremely low.

B: In an instance like the last one, can I assume the soul is simply getting the next available vessel as a parent?

L: Yes, that family or parent was the next in line.

B: Is it an aware soul that has more options available to choose a new living environment that would allow for success—like the concert pianist we talked about before?

L: Yes, but the option choice is no guarantee that the life to be led by the new soul will be "comfortable." The reincarnated soul may have the advantages to succeed as a pianist but also be lonely as a child or have parents who are not as loving. Understand that it all has to do with the lessons to be learned within the incarnation—again, there is a yin and a yang. The way to take advantage of any of this is to ascend and become more aware now.

More souls than you can imagine get caught up in a loop and reincarnate just about anywhere—I would say ninety percent of the current souls on your planet are in that position.

B: And your advice for a soul to elevate would be what?

L: It would be simple: you have to believe in yourself. Most humans run out of believing in themselves. If they do not believe that they can be better, they easily fall victim to your human frailties—crime, drugs, they harm, they damage, they destroy their own bodies and the bodies of others. They run the risk of becoming destructive because they do not believe.

B: Is there anything regarding reincarnation that I have not asked or that you think is important to share and essential for me to know?

L: Yes—that it will happen. Some do not believe in it; maybe they should. Everything is a cycle; everything spins and curves within the universe.

Let me share something not directly related to our discussion. Humans need others to hold them up because energy needs energy—that is why understanding the significance of the octopus analogy and all of your soulmates is important. You have to be structured that way; you could not deal with all of this without the support of the others. For example, Bud, there have been a hundred times when mates from your octopus head have sent you energy during difficult times, including me. We are all in this together for growth and advancement. As you go, so do I.

B: Please take a moment and relate that back to our discussion on reincarnation.

L: In a way, it does not relate back to our discussion directly because most humans will not get to the head of the octopus—they are just cycling through existing incarnations. It is very sad.

B: Is that because most of us are young souls with only a few incarnations?

L: Yes. Compared to the number of souls on your planet, there are very few advanced souls who are decreasing the number of octopus-appendage incarnations they have lived and are rising to a level where they can return their full energy to the head of the octopus and develop advancing reincarnation plans with the grand council members.

On the positive side of all of this, however, is time—with unlimited time, all things are eventually possible, both the yin and the yang. Reincarnation is a plan for all living things.

B: Regardless of their place of origin?

L: Not all. I was referring to the humans and animals on your planet.

B: Are you suggesting that there are beings that do not reincarnate?

L: Let's just say that the human soul is a very special thing—it is like finding a diamond in a rare area—some beings have it, and some do not.

B: In summary, Laz, this is extraordinarily different from any research or reading that I have done. Again, everything that you have shared tonight is far more complex than I could have imagined. Trying to make sense of it will be a challenge.

L: I have a final question for you before we stop. What is it that you have learned this evening?

B: I think it is what you have alluded to all along—that I have the ability to create my next reincarnation.

L: You are right. It all depends on what type of energy you apply to it. If it is love, kindness, and charity, it will give you back the same.

B: What is for next time, Laz?

L: We will talk about sound. I have to explain it in more detail. We talked about it before in *Soul Mechanics*, but there is a lot going on with sound within the incarnation process that needs further explaining. I think you will be surprised when I explain how it connects to breath.

This recent talk has produced a series of complicated perspectives filled with emotion, agitation, and confusion. They were generated by an accepted view of the afterlife melding with unconventional ideas, resulting in the formation of a picture that is contradictory to most modern beliefs of a soul life in the hereafter. My initial response? I am bouncing from one guardrail to the next, desperately seeking a place to settle my thoughts about what Laz has shared.

Ironically, my core reaction to what has been said is reminiscent of how, as a small child, I would wake up in the middle of the night and see everything in my room as unequally far off and distorted. I was frantic with youthful curiosity, and these clouded images gave the impression that they were leaking out from every angle in the room. As you might imagine, my state of mind about how a soul might be born again looks to be no different than those midnight encounters.

This afternoon I was standing on the back portion of my property, noticing a collection of menacing clouds rolling in from the west. During those moments, I was thinking about how thunderstorms erupt on occasion, stay for some time while I seek shelter, then move on. In comparison, my feelings about an afterlife soul world are similar—they attack me quickly and consume my thoughts for a marked period of time. Hopefully, these chaotic emotions will give way to a place of refuge.

The more I think about the process of reincarnation, I drift toward the origination, guardianship, and liability that each soul has in relation to the development of its next incarnation. As a result, I am being tugged in the direction of the prescription Laz recommended. Specifically, that increasing my awareness and attention toward love, charity, and kindness will modify my memories. If followed, I will have the antidote for developing any negative blueprint for my next life experience.

I can appreciate that the private evaluation of a soul's reincarnation process requires that all unconventional, story-bound possibilities be apparent before any plausible perspective is decided upon. Currently, however, to arrive at that position, I will need more time and a much longer period of serious contemplation.

Laz wishes to return to the topic of sound and how it affects the reincarnation process. To prepare, I will revisit *Soul Mechanics: Unlocking the Human Warrior*, where he first introduced the influence of sound on the soul.

CHAPTER 7

Vibration, Frequency, and Reincarnation

As I am preparing for my discussion on the impact of sound, I find myself securely trapped in the spiderweb of my soul counselor's interpretation of reincarnation. Here is my rationale for saying that: there are moments when my historical thoughts about how a soul might be reborn are like reading a time-honored, bestselling novel, whereas what Laz has presented appears more like watching an ill-fated horror movie.

Because of this, I am trying to avoid an emotional nosedive while frantically searching for a way to fasten what I have been told to an established anchor. I am hoping that this predicament may simply be the sudden absorption of new-found knowledge, and as a result, it is prompting unexpected angst.

Currently, this is my thinking regarding this personal controversy: In Buddhism, the process of moving from one life to the next involves my consciousness leaving the body at the time of death and entering an intermediate state, described as a very subtle form of being in which I have not entered my next incarnation. Apparently, in this state, I am propelled into my next rebirth by karma and the state of mind that I have developed over my life. There is no reference to the levels of review, the personal recalling of life memories, or the confrontation of all my historical thoughts—after all, Buddhists believe consciousness to be the property of the universe, not the human brain, something that I continue to agree with.

Regrettably, within the mystery of consciousness, jotting down observations, lists, and ideas does not come to me naturally. Therefore, nothing that I have learned can be optimistically modified, altered, or offered as a relief valve during any future late-night dinner conversation with friends or family.

Conceivably, however, I have a possible exit ramp as I get ready to discuss the spiritual effects of sound. While researching for *Soul Mechanics: Unlocking the Human Warrior*, I found that one of the most appealing paths to appreciate the mystical influence of sound was contained within the halls of theoretical physics. This came about through the merging of *string theory*—where all life elements are the vibrations of one-dimensional strings—and *the laws of vibration*—which dictate that everything moves and nothing rests, that we live in an ocean of motion.

Here is an example of how a real-world unification of these theories might influence how I can view sound. My Buddhist teachers have said that as the vibrations of sound move within a singular dimension, at times they are too delicate to be audible, making it difficult to be aware of many of life's most fragile tones. They also maintain that awe-inspiring sound is resounding within my inner being for all time. This becomes apparent whenever I attain a level of stillness within my focused meditation. Some of my Buddhist brothers have historically maintained that when immersed in intense conciliation and relaxation, there are moments when the implied manifestation of all sounds suddenly becomes audible. They have referred to this as the "great tones of life."

Outside the realm of science, a number of mystical, philosophical, and religious texts have spoken about the reckoning of all sounds and how a series of collective mystical echoes has gained access to their most honored traditions. For instance, Plato once wrote that the cosmos were constructed according to musical intervals and proportions, suggesting that everything was mathematically defined and precise. Comparatively, Lao Tzu described the Tao as "unimpeded harmony" and referred to the previously mentioned "great tones" as the creative resonance of all things.

Laz has already sanctioned the belief that sound and vibration were the accelerants that brought forward all creation. I suspect my soulful friend will build upon that notion.

Laz: Tonight, we will continue to talk about sound, but it will not be what you initially thought. I want to speak mostly about how all sound is frequency and vibration. First, I would like to do something.

Bud: What would that be?

L: Do this for me: look at the palms of your hands and tell me what you see.

B: I'm sorry—I don't really see anything other than my hands.

L: Believe for a minute that you are able to see your energy field—your aura. Now place your hands together as if you were going to pray.

B: OK.

L: Now, what have you just done?

B: Have I compressed the energy that you are referencing?

L: Exactly—you have created power. You may not know this, but this act is what the ancients did to generate maximum energy; now it is used only as a symbol for your prayers.

B: But how does this relate to sound and its effects on reincarnation?

L: We will get to that, but first we will talk about the frequencies and vibrations that you create, because that is the sound that needs to be discussed, not the noise that comes out of a human mouth.

B: Are you suggesting that the sounds I make through my frequency and vibration are more important than the sounds I hear?

L: Yes, but first, let me talk about the link of sound that you can create by "pressing" your frequency on another. A link of sound is when you have vibrated on somebody's level.

Say you have just touched the table in front of you, then connected to Shirlet by pressing her hand—at that moment, not only has your energy communicated with that table, but you have passed it on to Shirlet as well. You can do this through the "sound" of your frequency; further, what is happening to the table and Shirlet goes to you—it is like having a giant straw attached to both of you.

B: How do the parties involved interpret what is being transferred?

L: Your spiritual level of existence will determine all of that. If you walked up to a "magical" person and touched his or her shoulder, that person would automatically know that you have given him or her energy or that you have requested his or her energy. If you did that to a human whose frequency was not developed spiritually, he or she would think you are just a passing friend and would not assess an adjustment of energy.

B: An "energy-message" exchange only happens when there is a mutual or compatible level of frequency?

L: Exactly. You would still receive something from that person because of the energy link, but it would not be a mutual connection. Do you understand?

B: This transfer is a sound that exists but cannot be heard?

L: Yes, because vibration is sound—it is all one and the same.

B: Understanding this, is there a way that I could send a vibrational message to another individual without a physical connection?

L: Yes, especially if it were toward somebody who could receive it and know what it is. But if you were sending a vibrational message to John down the road, he might receive it but just think it is something outside. The question is, Would he or she acknowledge where it came from or what it was?

B: Without a verbal message, what does the receiver feel or sense at that moment?

L: The receiver would feel that something is off—like all sound just instantly stopped in his or her house. For example, did you ever hear the old saying that the crickets stopped in the summer night? That is because of passing vibrations.

B: With nothing to identify a vibration like that, does silence have the same effect as the frequency of sound?

L: Yes and no. Silence is shutting down. Silence is the mind and body void of color and connection, but it can never be void of vibration because you are energy, and energy is vibration.

B: Then, obviously, there would always be the existence of some form of sound—vibration, frequency—correct?

L: Yes. Here is an example for you to consider. Frequencies have the ability to make things solid, make things appear, open up gates, time travel; they can change your life, reverse your aging process, make you healthy, or make you sick. They can do anything because everything is made up of energy.

Here is another example. You call me Laz, but that is not my true name. My true name is a vibration of sound. All of us, all of our spiritual names, are made up of sounds—even the beautiful hierarchy of angels.

B: That makes sense in the context of your discussion about everything being energy.

L: Here is something for all of you to consider. Humans are the only species that name things, and even the names chosen include a vibration or musical tone. Think about something silly for a moment: say the word *perogies*—and say it the way that someone from that culture would say it. It has a musical tone, and in a way, it is that vibration that draws people to buy perogies.

B: You are right—that's funny but interesting. Are you suggesting that vibration and frequency can manipulate?

L: Actually, they can pave the path as to whether something goes right or wrong for someone.

B: Let me focus for a moment. How do the vibration and frequency of sound play out within the concept of reincarnation?

L: When you pass, that is all you hear. When you come out of the human shell, you have total knowledge of all the sound that is around you, and you vibrate with it. Most of the sound that you are vibrating with has to do with the frequency that you are attracted toward, and that depends on where your soul vibration is when you pass.

For example, if you have a high frequency and you have excelled, you can go into a position that humans refer to as heaven or a place created by higher vibrations. If you have a lower vibration frequency, then you would be attracted to a lower-level place. The level of your vibration syncs with a frequency and acts like a sucking device, drawing you into the vibration that you are attracted toward—it is like a magnet to steel.

B: Upon passing, I gravitate toward a similar or like vibration? Is that the "pulling" that people in a near-death experience feel?

L: Yes. Remember, however, your vibration is attracted toward whatever you developed while alive in this incarnation.

B: All of this ties back to the discussion of the seven heavens, the seven hells, and the levels of the aura—correct?

L: Yes. Everything is sound, and everything is vibration. Here is something to think about. Flowers sing: trees communicate—we hear them in spirit, but humans are not attuned to listen. Therefore, they do not hear any of this.

B: Is that why, immediately upon passing, the level of sound is difficult to tolerate—because we have been out of touch with these vibrational sounds?

L: Think of this—all of a sudden, upon leaving your shell, you can hear the water being turned on in all cities all at once. Think about all the computers in the world being turned on all at once—millions of them. Think about all the cars, millions of them. All the TVs being turned on, millions of them. Could you deal with that?

B: If not, how does a soul navigate all of that?

L: It is a shock to the system at first, and some souls are paralyzed for a small amount of time until they begin to work with their own frequency.

B: As you become compatible with your current life frequency, all of this becomes more manageable?

L: Absolutely.

B: If this is the impact immediately upon passing, how does sound play out with rebirth?

L: Still, everything is sound, and everything is vibration. You simply go through the vibration levels of incarnation.

B: I'm still a little confused. Let me set up an example. Let's agree that there are ten levels of vibration and frequency, with level zero being low and level ten being high. If my level is a five upon passing, then I would gravitate toward a level-five frequency path. When I reach the head of the octopus and decide to reincarnate, do I reincarnate as a level five?

L: Not necessarily. Try to follow this: if, hypothetically, you had your best life on the street in New York City and that was your happiest vibrational life, you could be attracted toward that past life and choose to go there within an incarnation for a while—but it is spiritually moving backward.

B: I am trying to follow what you are suggesting. Does this mean it could also work the other way, that a soul could move forward as well? If I am the level five that I just suggested, and in the life you just proposed I lived as a level eight, I could choose to gravitate toward a life where I knew I would be vibrating as a level eight if I so wished?

L: Why not? The soul will always try to search out a high point, especially if it has lower levels of vibration that it does not want to be sucked into.

B: As a result, can my soul be nurtured and grow within the past-life level eight I just referenced by choosing to reincarnate into the past life of a level eight?

L: If aware that it is possible, a soul can try.

B: I presume that is the trigger—that between death and birth, there is this awareness.

L: Sadly enough, yes. That is why I am telling you all of this—because, without that knowledge, the most recent path developed from the last incarnation is the one the soul is sucked into. Knowledge is power.

Let me explain further because I do not want you to be confused. You could reincarnate back to a more positive time, but you could not transfer that level eight to a new incarnation going forward. Do you understand? A direct link is always required in reincarnations moving forward. Remember, all time is happening now; you could go back within that time and embrace that vibration and frequency level, but you could not take that forward.

B: I get it. Any new incarnation that a soul plans is based on the most recent frequency and vibration from the last passing. In a way, the soul is always presented with its most recent learning and what may need to be addressed or corrected.

L: Yes.

B: Laz, a new soul coming to this place for the first time has what frequency?

L: They all start out as a level ten. Sadly, they then begin to work their way down because of the lessons on this planet—it is a school of sorts. Unfortunately, they could begin to commit the errors that we discussed in *Soul Sins and Regrettable Lies*. They come innocent, exploratory, and happy.

B: Have there been souls that arrive as a ten and leave as a ten?

L: Yes, but that is very rare. Those souls have the capacity to remove all grudges. It is all about maintaining a true frequency.

B: Can you take a moment and explain the frequency and vibration of a soul that is faceted and exploring multiple environments?

L: What would you like to know?

B: I am trying to move away from a singular soul-energy experience.

L: Think of all the vibration levels of sound as a learning experience. The frequency that they occupy is a learning experience. All the souls within your octopus head are learning different things from different frequencies—meaning different levels—but they are all vibrating in an attempt to be at one level, the self-level of existence.

B: So, all my faceted parts are operating at different vibration levels to learn about life from different angles—not all of them are fives or eights and so forth?

L: It is like all life; everything vibrates at different levels—houses, places of entertainment, people. Even you vibrate at different levels throughout the day.

B: And the way I say things also has the capacity to change vibrations?

L: Absolutely.

B: You were right in the beginning; I was not expecting this. I was not expecting such wide variations on the topic of sound.

L: Let me say this: humans have a very powerful weapon in sound—frequency and vibration—that they do not acknowledge. Ironically, it is both making them and breaking them.

B: Additionally, as you are suggesting, being unaware of the sound of human vibrations and frequencies plays out in the afterlife of a soul.

L: Think, for a moment, of the power of music. Even your scientists have acknowledged that musical vibrations can positively or negatively affect a plant—that powers exist everywhere.

B: Because of this, am I a walking musical machine?

L: In a way, yes. You are partially designed as an instrument— the output of this vibration is your human signature of who you truly are.

B: Is it the musical sounds that I make that attract or repel others?

L: That would be correct. The sound acts like a fingerprint registering within the other person, and vice versa. It is a program that you are feeding to the other people in your life.

B: The sound that we make is resonating within the human energy field that you described, and as we pass others, we are exchanging that energy?

L: Let's put it this way: as you pass another, there is an incredible exchange of energy information that a human is almost completely unaware of—all your information is picked up as you pass by the other people. Think of this connection and how unaware most are that it is happening—it is actually like the communication of a beehive that has been turned off.

B: Did we ever have an awareness of this connection?

L: Yes. There have been recent isolated cases of humans who maintained this level of connection—they were able to connect their vibration to the natural elements and make miraculous things happen, like walking on water. It all happened through sound and energy vibration.

B: Are these the "human warriors" that we discussed in *Soul Mechanics*?

L: Yes, they are—especially the ancient souls who have traveled here in the past.

B: We have covered a lot tonight—can you summarize the use of sound and its impact on reincarnation/afterlife?

L: Think of people who live in a crowded apartment building where they hear the people fighting down below them, all the traffic outside, and all the people on the streets—they have nothing but constant destructive sound. The impact of this has a physical effect on their health and on their vibration fields.

Conversely, you have Buddhists, whom both you and Shirlet have studied, sitting on the hill surrounded by flowers. They would not put themselves in the position of a crowded apartment because they are seeking an association with the pure sounds of nature so that they can heal and strive for a higher level of vibration. Even the physical sounds that they use in their temples, the sound of the gongs or singing bowls, are used for activation—the activation of the chakra fields, the activation of oneself, the activation of the other energies around them.

The difference regarding the approach to an afterlife in these two examples is the attention to the current human vibration and how that will play out in the next life.

B: What are your final comments on the sound created by frequency and vibration?

L: That would be easy—sound is life. Without sound, there would be no life, no color, no growth. There would be no communication between others. There would be no soul because it resonates within sound.

B: And to tie this back to other teachings, sound is breath?

L: Exactly. Every time you breathe, listen for the sound—because without it, you would not exist.

I have always believed that spiritual explorers should find a way to record their unique experiences and points of view. This endeavor has the power to deter unwanted emotional rubble when an accepted reality is obligated elsewhere. For me, it is a way to prevent skepticism and resistance from becoming the hallmarks of my life voyage.

As an example, here is how a newly formed soul guide explanation of sound (frequency and vibration) has the capacity to re-form my human cynicism. In the predawn quiet of any monastery visit, there will always be a moment of piercing sound. At about four o'clock in the morning, a resident monk will strike two gongs one second apart. They will sound two different notes—the second shorter than the first. The monk will then pause for just a few seconds and strike the gong again.

Slowly, the monastery will begin to stir (activate)—first with soft footsteps, then the rustling of clothes, but no voices (vibrating silence). Many of the resident monks will run to their appointed responsibilities while visiting laypeople file out of their rooms for an hour of morning seated meditation. Occasionally, a senior monk will organize "maverick visitors" who will choose an hour of walking meditation—quiet, measured steps forward, hands folded all within the vibration of silence.

When reassessing my history of monastery visits, I see innocent moments deeply hidden and set in voiceless motion—a vibrational link fashioned between the early morning frequency of an ancient musical device and the ensuing actions taken by others. While caught in the haze of these early morning activities, my brain might be perceived as mal-leable in nature, but the muted environment created by the vibration of silence galvanizes my otherworldly sensations. These are the instants when I am reminded of why Wendy Darling saved and stitched Peter Pan's shadow—they are the moments when I realize how my soul energy ties everything back to the human world.

There is still much more to learn from my soul guide Laz, and he has indicated that the process by which a soul makes the decision on a future incarnation is next on the list.

CHAPTER 8

Soul Life

*The uncertainty of any life is the brain
and ego's biggest challenge*
-Unknown

I once read that Einstein suggested that having an active imag-
ination was more important than knowledge, hinting that the
former required an obligation toward nonconformity. At this
point in my adventure, Einstein's recommendation may serve
as the prerequisite for undertaking any deeper voyage into a
realm of afterlife soul activity.

In being offered a banquet of alternative afterlife ideas,
I am presented with a next-world picture that is much less com-
fortably predictable than I would have anticipated. Ironically,
these troubled viewpoints may have lessened the burden of
my venturesome responsibilities by creating a new space for
me to mentally try out unconventional afterlife options. As
a result, my latest visit has challenged my ability to skip out
on the secret routines that my ego has tried to engrave on my

current incarnation. Mysteriously, I find myself welcoming that outcome.

Going forward, I am hopeful that with every passing spiritual encounter, it will get easier for me to cut to the chase regarding this afterlife adventure and apply the mental agility necessary to formulate an understandable post-life existence. Unfortunately, with everything that has been shared up to this point, I fear precisely the opposite—that there are times when I just may have an unyielding calcification of traditional spiritual values.

Those willing to research the life of a soul may find themselves forever trapped within the informative testimonies put forward by near-death experiences. As Laz has repeatedly submitted, NDEs only walk along the perimeters of an all-inclusive afterlife existence. Having been taken by surprise by this dilemma in the past, I accept that there is likely not one single, universally accepted human reality of an afterlife world waiting to be transcribed for all to embrace.

And what sits at the end result of my current debate? I am counting on a succession of continuing dialogues with Laz to marshal in helpful answers to any remaining questions that I may have about the world in which he resides. Realistically, there is no other alternative.

Bud: We have covered what happens when a soul passes and the multiple levels that it experiences in the past, but tonight you wanted to talk about soul life and the decision-making process to reincarnate.

Laz: All of that depends on the soul, does it not? It depends on the variations at the time and the soul itself. The soul needs several things before it starts making decisions. A soul always needs to have a past, a present, and a future. All three of these need to be copied all at once. Everything else is a "fill-in."

You have to be involved in all of the learning during an incarnation. How can a soul be learning about the past, present, and future if it is not existing within all three? To not embrace this would be narrow-minded.

When a soul envisions what is coming up within the next incarnation, it needs to see the total picture. Here is an analogy: it is like making a sandwich where you concentrate on the middle section, the meat and the cheese, but neglect the two pieces of bread. You have to experience the complete picture.

B: Walk me through this, because it is confusing.

L: Once you are located in the head of the octopus, you are in a position to create new versions of multiple soul experiences. The soul has newly formed energy, new tentacles of incarnation to be dropped, and new adventures to consider in the past, present, and future.

B: And these decisions are being made by my merged or complete energy?

L: Absolutely.

B: To be clear, when I am ready to reincarnate, do I have a clear path to create future multiple incarnations or "tentacles" around a learning experience of my own choosing?

L: Yes, absolutely. But remember, it will all be influenced by the karma you created during your most recent incarnation—the residual energy of all that occurred. If it is intense karma, you will have to first "ride that out" and see what you can learn or go back into those episodes to correct things.

B: Would it be possible to apply that historical karma to a new series of incarnations?

L: Again, remember—never think narrow-mindedly; of course, you can. Additionally, you can do that by choosing to reincarnate ten thousand years ago on this planet, ten thousand years ahead, or next year—all having the capacity to operate on different levels.

B: Based on the conscious decision-making of my soul?

L: Not always. Karmic events come into play, and also what the grand council would like you to experience. It is actually a dual decision made by you and those members.

B: Once I am fully prepared and informed, is that when my

energy is focused on what I will be designing for incarnations? Planning my next soul expeditions?

L: Once your energy is resolved and within the head of the octopus, you have the capacity to do a lot of things. One thing we have not mentioned, however, is the choice to have your soul rest. Most souls are exhausted when they reach that point. Think about how exhausting it might be to live multiple lives in multiple dimensions all at once.

B: Expand on that for a moment: How does a soul rest?

L: At the end of these incarnations, when the energy comes together within the head of the octopus, sometimes a soul will take more than a thousand earth years just to recuperate before any reincarnations are planned.

B: I do not mean to respond foolishly, but are there occasions when a soul might go on vacation?

L: It depends on what the soul thinks. For example, if the soul wanted to be on a beach, that is where that soul would be. The soul communicates with thought and travels at the speed of thought. When a soul is whole, its responsibility is only to the creator.

B: During an excursion/vacation, is the soul always regenerating its energy?

L: It needs to do just that. Some souls are so depleted from lifetimes of unplanned emotion that a period of hibernation is required.

B: You once shared that there is a crystal city that you visit. Is that a place for a soul to regenerate?

L: One hundred percent. It is a place to gain energy; plus, the soul needs to be in a position to be whole before it can start the process of copying itself and creating human shells. If it is not, then it runs the risk of bringing back the suffering, pain, and incredible loss that is still on its aura—the soul needs to cleanse itself.

B: While regenerating, the soul is also mapping out its next incarnations—correct?

L: Over time, yes, it will.

B: At this point, is the soul also interacting with its council for input? Also, is the soul interacting with the other soul energies, its soulmates, the other energies that reside within its octopus head?

L: How would you not be interacting with them when you have become one? You would be all-knowing at this point. It would be like this: You have a hand in one area, a leg in another, and so forth. Eventually, you become one—one whole body—so you would be interacting because you have become whole again. Think about and remember this: once you are there, you are interactively all-knowing, so it would make sense that you would know what the other energies are thinking and suggesting.

B: This is important for me to grasp. The five energies residing within my current octopus head, is that the energy that becomes whole?

L: You are suggesting something different. Your energy, that of Bud Megargee, is now whole and all-knowing and able to interact with the other housed energies.

B: I believe that I now understand. I can "socialize" with the other components of the octopus head if I desire to do so?

L: Only if you prefer it. Some souls prefer to go with their own thoughts and cleanse themselves for a time, and some do like the company of the others within the octopus head.

B: Once whole, are there occasions when I would "loan" some of my energy to one of the others within the octopus head?

L: You are not at that level, but a highly advanced soul would be able to assist other soulmates.

B: Once my incarnation plans are decided, my Bud Megargee consciousness is exclusively isolated to a new series of proposed experiences/incarnations, correct? There is no "car-ryover" to the other unplanned experiences or appendages?

L: Correct. Further, once you have concluded all of your dis-cussions about the multiple incarnations, all the tentacles are dropped at once to address the variations of the learning ex-perience. You would always be cautious so as to not fragment the soul any more than is required.

B: The recommended "master plan" is approved and then im-plemented; is it that simple? The cycle of incarnations starts over again—in multiple versions, worlds, genders, dimen-sions, and so forth?

L: There is so much that the soul desires to learn—multiple discrepancies are essential.

B: Laz, can you take a moment and summarize what we have discussed tonight?

L: That would be easy: the soul is a seed. Think about that for a moment. A seed is something that you put into the ground, and whatever grows comes back every year. For example, think about the flower—it comes back every year. It has a code built into it reminding itself that it is a flower, so it copies itself. It might have different-colored petals from time to time, but it is always a flower. The soul is a seed. It sows itself, sometimes at different dimensional levels. It is coded to know that it is a soul, so it copies itself and adapts to its environment to create the shell that is needed to function and thrive.

Ask yourself this: Why wouldn't something that is fashioned from the creator have multiple purposes? I would think that you might expect that to occur. It is like your country home—you have a room where you rest, a room where you hang out, a room where you cook. Certainly, a soul would have the same flexibility as your cottage. The soul creates a world so that the shell can function and thrive.

B: Laz, you have been teasing us all evening about carbon copies. Is that the topic for our next discussion?

L: Yes, but before we depart, I want you to try something. Do this for me—hold up your hand and imagine the function of each finger. For example, the thumb could be used to hitch a ride, the pointer finger to give direction, the middle finger to send a message, the ring finger for jewelry, and the small one for hand balance. Now, what about the palm of your hand? Could it be that your fingers are analogous to the octopus's appendages and your palm the head of the octopus?

One final comment: for a moment, think about the power that is created when you close those fingers and make a fist—that is similar to the power you have when your appendages/life experiences are completed, and your energy is whole within the octopus head. Perhaps that story will make more sense for some.

Tibetans have an expression for the challenge of maintaining a relentless mind while deliberating important transitory life issues: "tossing wood on the fire." Regarding my afterlife mystery, this is how I have interpreted that phrase. Generally, Buddhists believe that people go through life taking note of the life questions that routinely provoke their inability to stitch together both repetitive and unadulterated viewpoints at the same time. By adding unfamiliar and/or alternative information to the woodpile, they find change and flexibility where before there were undeniable, lifelong certainties. Essentially, they are exposing the building block for new points of view and untried opportunities.

As a result, the continuation of this afterlife journey has carried me to a similar point where the thoughtful consideration of abandoning historical soul-life beliefs might provide a departure ramp from my fictional ego death spiral.

Let me explain the previous statement further. My instincts have always led me to grab hold of what I know or what I find within my limited life experiences. This distinct, direct, and immediate perspective has always served as the initial concrete-dispensing device for my human ego. As an example, whenever threatened by a change in attitude or conviction, I struggle to quickly cement things back into place. Unfortunately, this only serves to provide another way of justifying the aspects of my personality that refuse to set adrift longstanding religious afterlife dogma.

My final thoughts, for now, I believe the wall protecting my ego debate is crumbling. With each passing session, it changes from an object to the process that shadows my tendencies for capturing and holding on to my previously fossilized ideas about the realities of a life after death.

Sadly, I believe that this predicament could be a feature of my current life karma—that today's spirit-world pursuits tend to coincide with what I absorbed in the past, and in so doing, my tendency to avoid change is heightened. The net result: perhaps my new spirit-world convictions are being pressed forward to the current moment—and like my soulful friend's version of a soul's hereafter plan, these new beliefs will begin "seeding" themselves.

As previously mentioned, to continue my spiritual expedition, Laz next wants to further address how and why a soul would "copy" itself.

CHAPTER 9

Duplicate Souls

I have concluded that in trying to salvage an unusual belief about an afterlife, I do not need to be so dramatic. What I mean to say is this: I have to be willing to quiet my mind and let go of my traditional ideas and what I believe to be absolute. After all, silencing an idea is an example of how it melts away. Additionally, consciously acknowledging the connection between ideas evaporating and what the spirit world unveils just might allow me to resolve the continuous cycle intended by the Theravada Buddhist principle of anatman, "no self/no soul."

Slowly, as Laz softens my mind regarding the preoccupation that I have with an endless series of questions regarding a soul life in the hereafter, my thoughts about the continuation of my personality become clearer—as Einstein suggested, my thinking needs to be bigger; I need to go beyond my current imaginings.

Following the most recent tape transcription, I find myself scrambling as fast as I can to return to the confined borders of the psychological and physical workings of my traditional world. It is only within this state that I can identify an accelerant for my continuing sanity and whether there may be a need for me to eradicate any forthcoming monsters that my spirit friend may reveal.

For that reason, I have concluded that Laz may be stirring sleeping giants that have been slumbering from the very start of this journey. To my surprise, I find myself welcoming the chance to see them in the light of day.

Recognizing how a soul copies itself should shed some light on how the soul-faceting process occurs—an action that has plagued my ability to understand how that might be possible.

Laz: I want to approach this topic in a completely different and unconventional manner. I would like you to think about how you would proceed with the following situation. Assume, for a moment, that you walk into a room with all the knowledge that you currently have, and you can see yourself sitting in a chair. Viewing yourself, what one word would you use to sum up what you see?

Bud: It would be difficult to come up with one word, but for this discussion, let's assume it would be *self-protecting*.

L: I was on that wavelength as well. So how would you help or assist yourself?

B: Through self-observation, evaluation, and insight?

L: I was curious about your answer. In many ways, I simply wanted to see how you would evaluate yourself because we will be talking about all of this tonight. I have asked this for a reason.

B: Does this relate to an exercise that we did following the last session, where you asked me to imagine the qualities of a higher version of my current self and a lower version? During that time, you were curious about my personal view of these possible examples. Following that evening, I imagined that in those scenarios, I saw my current self as both "self-protecting" and "overly cautious."

L: What would you say made you that way?

B: I believe that I would often stumble or delay in making some of my life decisions. Perhaps it involves not having the courage to make decisions because I was too concerned about what others would think.

L: Yet it is possible that the higher version of yourself could be more self-confident. If so, would you find it interesting when the current version of yourself and the higher version of yourself clash?

B: When I thought about the entire exercise, I often felt that any clash would always be formed within my current position—that as a higher version of myself became bold in decision-making, it might be filtered down from that hypothetical higher self, and any increase in passivity would be coming from the lower version.

L: Remember that at the end of our last session, I told you that we would be talking about copying. Well, we have already started with this discussion.

Now, go back for a moment. You are in this room with yourself, and the version that you are viewing does not have the advanced academic degrees that you possess or the insight into human existence. You, however, are aware that this is a lower version of yourself, and you are also aware of all the things that this version of yourself did. You clearly see that this version of yourself needs help. How do you proceed?

B: At first, I might try to examine all the ways that he became flawed, timid, fragile, indecisive, or tentative—all of his possible weaknesses.

L: Do you think that there are times when he might "overcompensate" and become overbearing and aggressive because of those weaknesses?

B: To balance out his weakness—perhaps. That may answer why a lower version of someone might excel in some areas of life despite the weaknesses.

L: Think of this for a moment: Think of every deficiency that he has as possessing its own desire. What would these desires want to do? Is it possible that they would want to be in control, which might lead that version of you to overcompensate despite the flaws?

B: Are you inferring that there is a balancing effect, that each flaw requires a counterpart—timid/strength, indecisive/bold, and so forth?

L: Absolutely. The lower version of yourself would want to get a "one up" on someone, and that could possibly come with some form of control.

Now, the higher version of Bud Megargee that you imagined . . . tell me more about him.

B: I suspect that he would likely show more strength and confidence, be confident and more unafraid in his decision-making—with a healthy sense of self.

L: Assume, for a moment, that both of those examples are operating at once. Now what do you think could happen?

B: Does the middle version get a combination of all that you have described?

L: And what would the end result of that mix be? Isn't it likely that you need to do an evaluation of yourself as having the possible outcomes of either side? If this truly exists, isn't that a possible outcome?

B: As opposed to just accepting that I am the middle component of multiple versions of myself? I assume the answer would be yes.

L: OK, so continue with that thought. Which copied version do you think is more dangerous to a soul's development, both here and in any possible afterlife?

B: The lower version, because of the flaws and negative karma that may result from that life?

L: Not true—they both contain some danger. Think about this: The higher version could become even more aggressive, and wouldn't that drag the others along with it in an effort to have all of the energy become one entity?

B: Are you suggesting that the middle version of myself in this example is the most vulnerable?

L: Perhaps, by getting lost in all of this and having its personality removed or drained from the total picture—your answer would be yes.

B: But with awareness, wouldn't it have the ability to appropriately assimilate the strengths and weaknesses one way or the other?

L: Let's examine that position—going back to where we started by having you sitting in front of that imagined version of yourself. What is the true evaluation of what you see now that we have discussed this?

B: I am a little lost. Before tonight, I would have said that I would be unaware of all of this.

L: And now the true evaluation of that version of yourself would be completely regrettable if you did not look at it as a component or reflection of yourself.

B: That all versions and all the strengths and weaknesses, regardless of the version—higher or lower—are simply me?

L: Exactly—they are you. Think of this for a moment: if you evaluated every set of circumstances in your current life this way, you would have all of your true answers.

This is our learning for tonight: everything has a copy of itself. I know it has taken some time to get to this point, but it is essential that you personalize this discussion so that when I go over the true evaluation of how a soul copies itself, you will understand how it cannot move forward with any selected purpose without having this kind of an evaluation. Without it, you would be walking into a darkened room with blinders on.

B: If this is true, then you are suggesting that just about everyone is unaware and blindfolded.

L: Blinded by themselves. They are the judge of their own judge and of their own hand.

B: Would being aware just produce more unused information if not acted upon?

L: Let's leap forward to the impact to try to answer that. When evaluating what a soul really is, where does your mind go?

B: In each of the examples, higher versions, lower versions, and so forth, there is a component of my energy grabbing a life position because of what is to be learned—some of which is not necessarily considered positive.

L: OK, if we have that portion of copying down and considered true, then how would you evaluate someone or some version of yourself in the future?

B: By considering all the possible levels of that person or version and not just the superficial levels that I am accustomed to seeing.

L: But what is the one single level that you are seeing? Could it be the higher level? Additionally, if the person or version does not say anything to you, how can you evaluate that person or version? What would you use?

B: Would it be as simple as maintaining an open mind toward the energy that the individual was displaying?

L: You are getting closer but go further with that thought. What would the evaluation actually be?

B: I'm not sure.

L: I understand your mental block because the real answer is that it would be chaotic. Would you like to know why?

B: Sure.

L: They are being copied. If there is a lower brain and a higher brain and they are constantly fighting for the lead, how could they not be chaotic?

B: But can I assume that the individual is not aware of this infighting?

L: Individuals are rarely aware. Continual awareness of this mix is not part of the current human makeup. As a side comment, look around your planet and tell me what you see. Would that condition be an example of a chaotic environment? Perhaps this could explain, in part, why that is happening.

Now let's take a deep breath. Think of your brain as if it were a power center—like a battery sitting in the middle of your head. This battery has two sides; one side provides positive energy, and one side holds negative energy. The trick to an effective evaluation and understanding a true copy of an individual would be in how you balance this positive and negative.

B: Yet, without awareness of what you have been discussing, it would be impossible to come to that conclusion.

L: Correct—that is your answer.

B: To back up for a moment, the concept that we are copies of ourselves is an essential vehicle to becoming aware?

L: Extremely, but also in terms of how you would handle and act on all of this.

B: I have no way of handling everything that you have just laid out. As a matter of fact, explaining any of this is sure to raise some eyebrows—it is certainly raising mine.

L: I am certain that is true, yet it is essential for both you and others to understand. In this life, you have to learn how to balance all of this in order to progress—especially once you are within the afterlife.

How do you balance a brain that is putting out a lower frequency and higher frequencies at the same time? How do you bring all of that together? This is why we started with you viewing yourself sitting in a chair in front of you, because that is what you would encounter.

B: I have no solid answer for you. I understand energy frequency and the need to continually balance that out, but the source of that energy is now under question with your current explanation.

L: To understand the afterlife, you need to completely accept that you are simply energy. Put that together with a universe of dimensions circling around your soul when it has passed and vibrating with all these different frequencies—it has to find a way to navigate and survive in that mess. How can that even become possible if you do not understand that a soul copies itself?

B: Certainly, to repeat myself, it would be awareness, but are you making the point that multiple incarnations are part of the formula for success? That there is no other mechanism to gain awareness within the human shell other than to have multiple opportunities and gain insight?

L: Now you are doing well. Multiple reincarnations are essential. Only a grand master—of which there are very few—can gain this type of insight without multiple lives.

Think of the soul as an incredible power center and the soul as a seeker of truths. The soul has to navigate all these different worlds, which would be encompassing all these different energies that we have been discussing, in order to learn and grow from them—low energies with terrible lifetimes and high energies with wonderful lifetimes. In the end, put it all together and compress it into one form of energy—at that time, you would be completely whole. That version of Bud Megargee is mind-blowing. Really, how many lives would a soul need in order to complete that picture?

B: Does this examination also explain why a soul needs to split like a diamond?

L: The bigger challenge is for you to fully explain soul splitting to yourself so that there is no question about its existence.

B: I have always expected that all I can do is ask the questions and try to digest what is explained to me. As you know, I struggle with much of this, but upon examination, I seem to find a place for it to settle—at least intellectually, if not emotionally.

L: Sadly, Bud, it is actually the truth, despite other teachings to the contrary.

B: Whenever we reach this point, I keep repeating to myself that old Buddhist phrase that we are far more than we imagine ourselves to be.

L: Do you know why they say that? It is more than simply explaining that everything is transformational. Here is something to ponder: What if I told you that you are that couch you are sitting on—that you are the energy that you breathe? What if I told you that you are a creator and, in a way, a god—not the master creator/God but one with capabilities to construct a life? There is so much involved in all of this—that is why we are having all these discussions. Your true reality is much greater than imagined. The true reality is for one to realize the greatness of oneself.

To summarize, your true power comes with the ability to focus and stabilize the positive and negative energies with a single thought—that is where your real soul power comes from.

B: Does a soul know what we are discussing before coming to this place? And wouldn't that have been thought out during the afterlife examination?

L: You did know it, but as a soul, you never "lived it," and that is how a soul learns, by mentally, emotionally, and physically experiencing all of this.

B: And the role of the human ego?

L: The human ego loses its influence whenever you tap into your potential.

B: Can you bring all of this back to the issue of soul copying, which is where we started?

L: Consider this for a moment. Ask anyone to pick up two cushions from a couch and explain the differences and similarities of each and why he or she came to these conclusions. Most would describe the shape, color, makeup, and so forth. Very few would indicate that there was a probable transfer of energy based on what we discussed earlier. Maybe it was picked up by someone who was brilliant, and a small portion of that energy was transferred. Most would evaluate—like you did with the earlier exercise—by simple visual evaluation, not looking at the possible levels beyond what the human eye sees.

B: Are we just unaware, or are we lazy?

L: The brain is not being taught to see beyond the obvious.

B: Are you suggesting that with time and patience, anyone can learn to peel away the obvious superficial layers we have been talking about?

L: Individuals can develop the capacity to peel away the layers and see who they truly were and why they were copied. Let me give you a true example—the leaves on a tree. Have you ever really noticed the leaves of a maple tree? Are they all the same or different? If they are all the same, why would that be the case? Looking at it with superficial eyes, you would probably say they are all the same. But why can't they all be different shapes—squares, rectangles, and so forth? Why do you think that a tree would make multiple copies of its own leaves? Was that a choice of the seed that grew that tree?

B: Obviously, it would not be to simply show a difference when compared to other trees.

L: The answer is camouflage. As an example, assume that leaf number five thousand did something wrong. Are you going to find it? Probably not.

B: Take that analogy and apply it to a human.

L: OK. With a human shell, they all generally have two eyes, two legs, two arms, two ears, and so forth—why is that the case? And why would they camouflage? What would the purpose of that be? What would your evaluation be?

B: I am lost.

L: The reason energy copies itself is to stabilize itself.

B: To balance—the analogy about the battery. The contrast of life—good/bad, right/wrong, and so forth. Without copying a single life—higher or lower—it could run amok.

L: Yes, exactly.

B: To try to understand where you have gone with all of this—the fact that there is variance in the higher, lower, and same versions of myself, the copies, has to do with balancing out my soul? And can I assume that there are many more variations of myself than we have discussed tonight?

L: Yes. So next time when you look at a tree, remember that one leaf could have done something, and if you looked at that tree superficially, you would never find it. The same applies to you or anyone else for that matter.

B: I have a question as a result of your analogy. These differences within the versions of a soul, do they provide for "learning experiences" as a "required" part of an incarnation?

L: If you think about all the trees that have different-colored leaves, different sizes, and so forth, what happens?

B: Does it give a wider range of tree energy and a sense of individuality?

L: Yes, that would be robustness. But what else? It would also give it the chaos we talked about earlier. All the differences create a lower vibration field—everyone trying to be an individual.

B: Chaos is an integral component of an energy's existence? Essentially, you cannot have the robustness and individuality without a chaotic environment?

L: To a point, it is essential—but the negative chaos, not so much. Now, examine that earlier version of Bud Megargee. Within his brain, he has both upper and lower—positive and negative—energies, not unlike a forest filled with trees. In your current incarnation, and assuming you are the middle version, you would be the trunk of the tree.

If the trunk simply tries to extend its energy out to influence control, each leaf that would be like a human trying to reason with the chaos that surrounds him or her. How does that generally work out?

B: Within the afterlife, is all of this part of the "blueprint" of a next incarnation—variations, upper and lower, and so forth—and within all of this, there would be copying?

L: Your answer is yes. What needs to be understood is that everything is copied—that it has an image, and there is more within that image than what your eyes see. Sadly, what you see with a simple view is not the "real" image. The real image is the complexity of a soul's ability to copy the complexity of a soul's energy system. One of your Buddhist teachers once told you this when he said, "Some things are true but not real."

For the people who have had the ability to see or take pictures of a soul, what did they see? They see an orb—all souls are round orbs of energy.

B: Why is that?

L: Because they are copied. And the differentiation between the multitude of souls is their vibration and frequency, but yet in the beginning, you are all photocopies of one another. The "personalities" that you speak of come as a result of the incarnation that each soul has and the energies—positive and negative—that it experiences during those lives.

Now imagine looking at a soul sitting in a chair, as you

did in the beginning with the lower version of yourself. You would not see the "differentiation" of frequency and vibration if you were viewing it with superficial eyes.

Within the world of souls, it is the energy that becomes bold in its incarnation decisions that transforms and moves forward—the humans who care more about developing themselves than pleasing those around them. When you arrive home this evening, take a moment and think of the humans who have placed a helpful mark on this world. In doing so, they created a type of positive chaos. It came as a result of their balance.

B: I need some assistance from you, Laz—there is so much for me to think about tonight, and frankly, I am exhausted, but I would like to plan for next time. What will we be talking about?

L: I would like to talk about why souls choose a human shell, the process of being connected to the human world—why the soul is choosing various types of shells. I would like to go over every part of the transformation that occurs from being a soul to occupying a human body and how the incarnation plan is developed.

I have tried to find refuge over the past few days so that I could take a hard look at both my opposition and my storybook obligation to the unusual message about soul copying that Laz had shared. Ironically, I knew from the beginning that entertaining a mysterious voyage into the world of souls would create convincing waves of uncertainty, but I did not expect to find myself in the riptide of such strong waters.

Clearly, I am wanting to unmask something from the untouched corners of the world that my spirit friend inhabits. Unfortunately, I do not believe that I will ever find it while using an established toolbox of standard reasoning.

Here is an example of what I am talking about: what I am experiencing while navigating this colorful afterlife picture is beyond words and cannot be easily processed by an unadventurous mind. Like most people, I have been encouraged to learn and think in dualities: truth versus lying; risk versus security; living versus dying. Subsequently, when I encounter experiences that do not fit within these distinctions, I almost immediately toss them away. They make me anxious, and I often run for cover. Perhaps I am being directed to a position where it is the belief in nonduality that creates human awareness.

Following this latest discussion, I find that developing an awareness about duplicate souls is like looking through a kaleidoscope as it rotates, a constant stream of altered angles. Laz presents the importance of awareness as if it were the nourishment that is required to allow a deeper level of transcendent wisdom to flourish. My hesitancy in fully embracing such a view is to prevent my current existence from being fractured. I do not want to be impulsively attaching myself to a particular experience, especially one that relates to an alternative form of spiritual awakening or understanding.

At this point in my journey, I have become completely unsettled. I say that with the understanding that explorers of unconventional events willingly accept that there will be rough moments that are occasionally balanced with peaceful exuberance. Occasionally, this enthusiasm might become spoiled, yet an explorer's optimism is never weakened by personal insecurities. I find myself scrabbling for those moments.

This journey was never planned as a theatrical project where historical beliefs would be challenged but protected. Realistically, I understand that old beliefs die hard, but occasionally, some do, in fact, die.

I will find a way to resolve any ongoing awkwardness regarding how souls originate and continue to duplicate throughout their existence, but for now, I will prepare for my next soulful encounter—the act of transforming from a soul to a human shell.

CHAPTER 10

Soul Transformation— Becoming Human

As I gain more insight into the shadowed qualities of the spirit world, I seem to find more faith in accepting the limits of my human understanding of an afterlife reality. Further, I am beginning to see that my historical understanding of the complexities of soul reincarnation might have been secretly protected by my human ego. As a result, the more experiences that I have while discussing afterlife possibilities with spiritual surrogates and others, the easier it becomes for me to effectively unpack all of this.

Going forward, I believe that Laz might be adjusting these discussions in an effort to enable me to one day wake up to a different afterlife reality. An existence in which I can actively adjust what might come next upon my human passing. A spiritual existence that is completely absent of attachments to faulty conclusions or age-old beliefs that I have considered inevitable.

Temporarily, my feelings about this afterlife journey have shifted, and I have become more curious than anxious. For example, I wonder if my initial viewpoints about this other-worldly exercise are solid enough to absorb a punch to the stomach—one that not only knocks the wind out of me but is also strategically placed in such a way as to forever alter my future understanding of a soul's eternal life.

With everything that has occurred up to this point, when I sit in quiet isolation, my thoughts drift to the magnitude of opportunities that might exist upon any one of us passing. Moreover, if there is a sliver of truth to these discussions, the level of personal responsibility within my current reality could be beyond crushing.

Once more, Laz has pointed out that the quality of an afterlife is conditionally based on the frequency developed and amplified through every thought and action while living. He is relentless on this point, and because of that, he is making it difficult to safeguard any of my long-established religious beliefs.

Regardless of any remaining feelings that I have on these matters, I will examine how a soul takes on form in our next discussion. I believe that I may be coming close to finalizing this debate—after all, once back in human form, the afterlife cycle has been fulfilled.

Laz: We are going to talk about the act of reincarnation tonight, are we not?

Bud: Yes. Specifically, I would like to examine what occurs

after a soul has completed its afterlife journey and chooses to incarnate as a human again.

L: I want to do this—but absent of any narrow-mindedness. You need to remember all that we have discussed involving balance.

Let me recap for a moment: the biggest thing that happens when a soul leaves the human shell is that it seeks to cleanse itself—it has a lot of baggage or karma from its most recent human incarnation. Without removing or adjusting this, it would be impossible to ascend and consider a future reincarnation to a higher dimensional level of existence.

B: This is my question about what you just said: Does that soul have a clear awareness of what is required to complete a total cleansing so that it can consider a new human life?

L: As we previously discussed, such awareness occurs only after you face the process of completely reviewing your past life episodes. Typically, humans can glance at their reflections in the mirror, but they don't really look deeply into themselves, do they? They mostly want to look presentable to others—not at their true selves.

B: Is that something the human ego blocks during this life?

L: It is easy for the human brain to be superficial and take that position. Ironically, if a human could look into that mirror and witness his or her true earthly actions for twenty-four hours—that would result in a "true hell." Without a complete cleansing, the soul could be stuck in the same position over and over.

B: Regarding most human incarnations, what is the one learning that would be absolutely required to finalize any cleansing and avoid this repetition?

L: Easy—patience, combined with balancing yourself. For a moment, think of an angel trying to fly with one wing. How far would that angel get?

B: It would be traveling in a circle.

L: Absolutely, and so would any soul that is unable to remove all its karma baggage. The question that you need to answer is this: What baggage do you possess that needs to be adjusted now before you pass? Or what baggage has been balanced, if any?

B: Are you suggesting that I have failed to balance out how others think and feel toward me?

L: Yes. Without clearly identifying all of this, the karma continues.

B: Let's back up for a moment. Imagine that I have successfully balanced and cleansed all of my baggage, I have returned to the head of the octopus, and I am a complete energy. Now, how do I go about constructing my next incarnation and making the selection of the souls I might be interacting with?

L: At that time, you would have come to a dimensional level that was higher than your last incarnation because you would have been completely cleansed. You would have ascended. You then start to review what went right or wrong in the past incarnation—everything would be considered by you and the council. Also, a location would be considered where you could do better—where you could do the best work that is needed on the planet. Then you would be selecting everything you need to make that happen. Sometimes you can choose your own family, and you could be reincarnated with those souls. Essentially, you would have completed all the "research" that would be required for a next life.

What you might find interesting is this: Some negative souls—complete with their historical karma baggage—travel to a lower vibrational level and do not ascend to a place where they could choose the next life. They could go into a reincarnation process determined by others and bring back all of their negative traits. Essentially, they are living a life similar to the one they just left.

B: Are these souls caught in an evolutionary soul loop?

L: They are caught in a version of a soul hell that they created by themselves. Here is an example. Assume for now that a soul has done some very terrible things, and that soul passes. That soul would be at an extremely low vibration level upon entering the spirit world and would be experiencing a self-imposed hell while being held accountable as it passed through the seven senses along with the seven heavens and seven hells. The powers of the soul world would allow the reincarnation to occur, knowing what that soul is bringing into its new life—all of its uncleansed karma baggage from not having learned from its past-life experience.

B: And that is "allowed," despite the inability to remove negative energy from that past life?

L: Is there evil in your world? It is not a matter of allowing—everything is mandated by energy, vibration, and frequency. Everything is about what you put into it. Think of standing in a circle of fire and seeing a number of red doors—all numbered. Think, for a moment, that you have to go through every door and have a lifetime, and every one of those lives has baggage that you will accumulate. Based on all the deeds that you have built up from going through those doors, you will either ascend up or move downward, and any unremoved energy will go with you into your next life. It is the same as we discussed with the octopus analogy.

B: Let me take this discussion in a different direction momentarily. When a soul decides to reincarnate, complete with a direction, a new life, a new family, and so forth, do the souls that are to be attached during this new incarnation agree to accompany this soul, including those negative souls you just mentioned?

L: They are not always in agreement—especially if they are at a higher or lower frequency. Some of your life encounters are predetermined if you picked them, especially if you were in a higher, cleansed position to do so.

Think of this—think of being a human. In a day, what do you need to live?

B: The essentials like water, food, and shelter.

L: You would also need companionship—someone to mentor or teach—so it is up to you to pick the right people to provide that in life. There is one caution with this approach, however. The people you choose will assist in the lessons you will learn, and that alone might bring others into your life. They also will bring additional learning—some of them may be the negative souls we mentioned earlier.

B: So essentially, I am putting together a learning team.

L: Correct. And you will rub some of the people you encounter the right way; with others, you will rub them the wrong way. And as we have discussed, the ones you have rubbed the wrong way will become baggage that you will carry in your energy field and potentially to your next afterlife review.

B: Can I assume that the negative baggage and the exposure to potential negative souls are part of the yin and yang of life?

L: Not necessarily for everyone. Souls who repeatedly cause harm or conduct their lives for evil purposes—do you really think that they are learning from those actions?

B: In the case of negative souls, can a soul become more aware, break negative cycles and leave the baggage?

L: Exactly. Both continue until that soul comes across someone or something that gives it a road to where the soul can learn to be different. Put this in the current context of your planet: Could this be why you have so many souls in your prisons? And from our discussion this evening, what would the primary answer be to change this cycle of behavior?

B: Could it be what we started with this evening—balance?

L: Correct. What if, for example, in one day you performed some dubious acts out of anger or the absence of control, and each time you did that, you were instructed to carry fifty pounds of concrete—how long could you continue to carry that weight?

B: Are you suggesting that I do not account for the fact that I have done this every day?

L: Yes, I am. Now, think of all the souls that do not realize what we have just said. Most people you meet will never know about what we just discussed. Yet you see how critical it is for afterlife review and the selection of a next-life incarnation.

B: I don't want to divert too far from this portion of the discussion, but I do have many remaining questions before we go further into this incarnation process.

L: Yes. What would they be?

B: For example, what is the purpose of a soul—positive or negative—incarnating and then dying early, as a young child or infant?

L: There is no specific purpose. It might have the distant purpose of teaching something to the others around it, but otherwise none. It has everything to do with the totality of the environment that the soul is born into. Remember that for a question like this, the human response will be different from the response that would be coming from the soul world. Humans see that a soul life was interrupted—we see it differently.

B: Is the difference connected to the "life plan" set into motion by that soul?

L: Sometimes, if a soul does not want to be reincarnated but is required to, that soul will fight against it. Environment plays a role in this, as does a soul's past life. For example, if a soul died of an illness and is still carrying that baggage along with its pain and suffering, that soul could reincarnate with that illness—that is why some children are born with an illness.

B: If this is true, then are those souls falling victim to the reincarnation-loop problem?

L: That loop can become a never-ending cycle that continues. Remember the circle of fire and all those doors—you can gather quite a bit of negative baggage over those incarnations, and typically not all of it will have been balanced, if it was even known.

Bud, there is no perfection—even with the souls that have the best intent. Each reincarnation has the possibility for a soul to choose a family and geography that would not be the best choice or place for a new life.

Here is an example of what I am trying to relate to you. Say you are a young soul, and you are about to enter into a new baby's body. You picked out your family members—all of them, including grandparents. All of those souls are on this planet for what they need to accomplish, and they are working through and trying to cleanse both historical karmic ties to the past and recently accumulated baggage. Additionally, they have something good and something bad—yin and yang—around them. What are the odds, at that point, of removing trauma from the next incarnation?

B: Does the incoming soul know that all of this baggage

exists within these selections and that it is expected to navigate around these challenges?

L: Within the world of souls, your answer is yes. Sadly, when you die and come out of your human shell, your psychic ability to perceive things is at one hundred percent, but when you are reborn, most of it is lost.

B: New souls are not aware of future circumstances once they are in a newly formed human shell?

L: Only the highly advanced and mature souls—souls with completely open abilities.

B: Are they the souls that you described as "human warriors" in *Soul Mechanics*?

L: Yes.

B: These variables are very complex. It seems to me that almost anything can happen from incarnation to incarnation.

L: Yes.

B: One point of clarification: Is it possible that I could complete a full cleansing, arrive at the head of the octopus, and plan an incarnation, yet still have an advanced soul or creator intervene because it feels that a certain learning should take place?

L: Yes. An advanced soul would, in part, intervene to avoid having a soul select a very easy life plan, which would result in much more difficult plans later. Again, it is a subtle form of balancing. On the other hand, there are times when you need to be placed in a difficult position because only then can you become a stronger soul.

B: Is this an attempt to encourage an advanced soul to take risks?

L: I do not think any advanced soul would look at it that way—some still think of incarnations as a form of hell. I say this despite the fact that an advanced soul realizes that difficult challenges are always forthcoming.

In addition—there is a very real possibility that a "life learning" would encompass a series of repetitive experiences so that a soul would grasp the full intensity of the learning. As an example, could it be possible that you have been both doctor and patient over and over so that you would learn everything about emotional disturbances?

B: That makes sense to me.

L: You learn from both sides of an experience.

B: In an effort to bring this back to the octopus analogy, the higher versions of these learning incarnations would be at the upper levels of each octopus tentacle—in essence, within your explanation, the higher versions of the soul's energy, correct?

L: Yes. Isn't it interesting that with multiple hearts and multiple brains, so many variations and complexities surround this sea creature? There are hidden reasons for the use of that analogy. Let's just say for now that certain creatures are not just here to swim around and be eaten as a delicacy. I will share this with you at this point: the ancients looked at this quite differently.

B: Are you suggesting that an octopus uses more of its natural, intended, innate gifts than we do as humans?

L: Think about that for a moment. They are not as advanced as a human, but they do not let anything stop them from growing a limb or modifying their environment—they just believe that they can. I find it interesting that they have no doubt. It is a creature that was never taught that it could not do those things. Can you say that about the human race?

B: I am going to take a wild guess here. With what you are alluding to with this analogy, are you suggesting that a soul residing within the head of this octopus, once whole and fully cleansed, never questions what it is capable of doing once it decides to reincarnate—there is literally no doubt?

L: Now you have it. And there are other similarities that make it a fitting creature to describe soul life.

B: Before we talk about that, let's circle back to the incarnation process before I get too lost in what you just said. You stated that a soul might be required to reincarnate against its will. Why would that happen?

L: Because it might have to incarnate to save another soul who is important for the planet, or it might need to come into form to make a difference on the planet or because a situation is required to learn.

B: So, some souls can be "recruited" for certain events?

L: Absolutely. And those events could be both positive and negative in nature.

B: Would a soul resent being incarnated to attend to a negative event or to participate in a negative life?

L: Not necessarily, but some souls are tired of incarnating, regardless of their vibration level or frequency. These souls might harbor an attitude. Think of this—think of the people who say they were born in the wrong era or talk about how they just do not want to be here. In rare cases, some will try suicide to get off the planet, or they use substances to block out the entire experience of the incarnation. They have no desire to advance into a different reality.

B: Would it be accurate to assume that the creators you referenced earlier use a different set of guidelines for souls that are hesitant to incarnate or display resistance?

L: On occasion, yes. From a human perspective, death is disturbing and sometimes painful, but from a soul perspective, being born is twice as bad. You are reincarnated in a very small and vulnerable shell, and you are completely reliant on whomever you are reincarnated with for your every need—your existence. Anything can happen to you because there is no control. Who would want that?

Let me give you something that has never been mentioned and is likely to be difficult for anyone to accept. When an advancing soul (an energy that has arrived in the head of the octopus) has reincarnated and lying in the hospital crib it is trying to communicate with the other souls in a clairvoyant way. Unlike a soul that is in a reincarnation loop, an advanced soul is intimately aware of its past lives, and here they are now, trapped in the newly created shells.

B: So that I may understand what you have just suggested, take me deeper within that voyage. Once the plan is implemented, I am injected into the newly created body during pregnancy, correct?

L: Any time before the birth, yes.

B: Do I arrive within the new body instantaneously?

L: Yes.

B: Then I immediately start merging with the brain of the infant?

L: It feels like a vacuum—you are totally pulled into it.

B: Is this process easy, or does the brain fight this?

L: Sometimes it is quite easy because the subconscious mind is not developed enough to start thinking on its own to stop it. If, however, the incoming soul is at a higher and more advanced level of vibration and frequency and does not want to incarnate, then there are going to be issues. That could be one of the many reasons some would lose children—because the soul is fighting it all the way.

B: Do souls eventually find a comfort zone with each new transformation into an incarnation?

L: More so, the comfort zone is found when it is understood that the mother and father actually want the child to be born. Conversely, the new soul has a continuous fight if they do not.

B: Here is my question with all of this: The new life consciousness created by the merger of the incoming soul and the new human body, is that the consciousness that passes upon death? In other words, the new life learnings are integrated into the soul's consciousness and total energy?

L: Yes. The shell simply dies off—it is like the computer has been shut down. Think of it this way, as if it is a car, and the brain is the engine and the soul is the gas—without it, you have nothing.

B: Let's go back to the nursery example you related. Could you explain in more detail this period of panic and confusion that a soul experiences?

L: Assume, for a moment, that you are an advanced soul with all of its cleansed energy. If you were to pass tonight what do you think would happen? You would find yourself lying in a hospital crib, remembering the fact that you, Shirlet, and I had this discussion—you would remember all of this current life that you are experiencing and wonder, "What happens now?" You would feel terrified, vulnerable. You would wonder if people knew that you were now in this nursery—whether people in your past life were looking for you. Everything would hit you all at once. Just imagine knowing everything that you know at this moment and waking up as an infant in that crib—how do you think you would adjust to that?

B: Essentially, feeling trapped?

L: Yes, because you are—you are in a very vulnerable body.

B: Does every new soul experience this?

L: To a degree but not to the level of an advancing soul—and it always wears off.

B: I find it remarkable that every newly reincarnated soul has a mechanism to communicate this uncertainty.

L: Some souls can remember portions of their soul life for a period of time, and then it starts to fade with an everyday existence within the new life. It wears off around age five or six.

B: Does this answer the questions about a young child's "special friends"?

L: Many times, these are members of the soul's last family who have not reincarnated yet. Other times, because the new soul's third eye is wide open, that soul is seeing recently passed souls.

B: Why does this skill wear off?

L: Because of the control that all of you experience on this planet. It is not something that this life was meant to encourage. Your awareness becomes where you are. People stop their awareness because of this life, and sadly, it was never designed that way. You were designed to be all-knowing and all-encompassing and go further than where you are, not stay in your bubble.

B: Earth's conditioning is the main factor in the removal of the awareness?

L: Yes.

B: With everything you have just described, it raises one

important question: Why would souls choose to come to a place like this?

L: Because there are times when the choice is made for them; other times, they are up for this type of challenge; and then, of course, there are souls that choose not to incarnate altogether—they would certainly avoid a place like this. There is an unlimited number of ways to learn lessons—or not learn them. The life choices available for a soul on this planet are far more creative in terms of learning options than other life options could ever be.

B: Laz, one thing I am taking away from tonight is the enormous variability of possibilities—it seems endless. As a result, what can a soul do now to make the odds better in terms of avoiding confusion and moving forward in an effort to ascend above all of this?

L: That is why we started with the issue of balance—that is your answer. Nobody is perfect, but you do need to become more balanced.

B: I am drained. Laz, can you give me a quick summary of the adjustments a soul needs to make prior to inhabiting a human form?

L: It is very simple—it is about building blocks. It is about becoming aware of everything that you were when human—having an awareness of the good and the bad and understanding all of that. There has to be a balance within your subconsciousness because you are creating your next shell and where you will live within that shell—your world, your decisions. You are literally building it; you are developing a plan as you sit here in front of Shirlet and me. Being balanced prior to coming into that plan will prevent any "life rocks" from falling.

So, an awareness of what you have done up to this point will put you in a better position to build your next soul event on this planet. It all comes from regaining the strength of the subconscious mind and creativity—then you will be able to enhance the planet by coming in with love.

B: If a soul is reasonably successful with what you have just stated, does that make the next incarnation easer to embrace?

L: Not completely, because while in spirit form, the subconscious mind still has a memory, and you will still remember who you were and what you did. The outline designed while in spirit form is silenced by the incarnation amnesia. Like I said before, most of you take on the new incarnation in the rawest of forms.

B: OK—I am done. What can we expand on for next time?

L: There is only one way to go, and that is to talk about transcendence and how a soul gets to that point—essentially, how to build an insurance policy for your next life.

*Let us prepare our minds as if we'd come to the very
end of life. Let us postpone nothing. Let us balance
life's books each day . . . The one who puts the finishing
touches on their life each day is never short of time.*
—Seneca

There is an intriguing ancient story that, when translated, reads something like this: Upon returning home after major military victories, triumphant Roman generals were paraded through the residential streets to the uproar of approving and adoring crowds. This regal pageant more often than not covered the course of an entire day, with the celebrated generals riding in the most stunning chariots. The returning battle-weary warriors were literally hero-worshipped by both the legions they led into combat as well as the everyday citizenry lining the streets.

There is an odd part to this historical narrative that I find noteworthy. Riding in the same chariot and standing just behind each general was a slave, and this person's sole task throughout the entire procession was to continuously whisper in the general's ear, *"Respice post te. Hominem te esse memento. Memento mori,"* meaning, "Look behind. Remember thou art mortal. Remember you must die."

As you might expect, this ceremonial tradition was intended to remind all revered Roman soldiers of the instability of life and that moments of triumph should be *balanced* with a perspective that instilled a universal form of humility. In truth, the implied message was that life is fleeting—that all temporary earthly glorifications end, yet the truth of one's life and actions is fixed for the remainder of time.

I imagine the message disclosed to both the admiring crowds as well as the generals themselves must have been a torso-throbbing testimonial for the significance and unpredictability of all life. That there is great flexibility, yet little distance, between the confidence of an ascending warrior's victory and the ensuing residue (baggage/karma) formed from the terror inflicted on a conquered people.

Besieged by the reaction to the new information from my most recent evening's discussion, without warning I found myself both beautifully optimistic and terrified. To my surprise, a close friend took it upon herself to compare my mindset to that of a nomadic feather—one that is endlessly being tossed by the wind, complete with a brisk and ever-changing angle of the reality of a hereafter. My comeback to her was framed with the recognition that everything I had known about an afterlife was now in perpetual motion and frantically haphazard. Nothing had crystallized into an accepted position, except that I had been left in an uncertain and inexplicable state. Clearly, on the question of life after death, I was not balanced.

In the end, I reread my notes from this somewhat bizarre evening and concluded the following: I believe that once I move from my dogmatic beliefs to an understanding that all things are impermanent, the tension between my expectations about a life after death and the reality of what an afterlife might actually entail will begin to evaporate. Arriving at that point, I can appreciate that the unexpected emotional annoyances I continually feel will slip away and that the questions I have been seeking to satisfy will be easily answered with one simple phrase: everything adapts with awareness and balance, even the life of a soul.

My next meeting with Shirlet is to explore the spiritual notion of transcendence. I believe my expedition into the unfamiliar world of souls is slowly coming to an end—unless, of course, Laz has other plans.

CHAPTER 11

Transcendence

As I neared the end of my graduate studies, I began to think about the conditions I might have to navigate on the way to incorporating the discipline of humanistic psychology into my overall analytical training. As a result, I, along with a core of equally adventurous grad students, blocked out my weekends and enrolled in every available humanistic psychology seminar at the Eastern Pennsylvania Psychiatric Institute (EPPI) in northwestern Philadelphia. It was there that I took my first deep dive into the forward-looking theories of Erich Fromm, R. D. Laing, Rollo May, and Viktor Frankl, just to name a few. After every class and exercise, I inhaled their theoretical texts and academic letters, all in an effort to engross myself in a freshly expanded view of "wholistic" psychology.

During these early training conferences, with the romanticized remnants of the 1969 Woodstock festival still firmly entrenched in my mind, the topic of nonchemically induced "self-actualization" often consumed our therapeutic after-hours debates. With the possibility of a natural and capable road map of personal improvement alive in all of us, I accepted one surefire fact: Abraham Maslow's text *Motivation and Personality* and his theory of a hierarchy of needs had outlined exactly how I could move toward the goal of becoming self-actualized.

Over time, I began to realize that all the weekend participants essentially perceived the concept of Maslow's self-actualization through the lens of their familial values. Yet in spite of those imposed diverse pressures, at the core, we were all very similar. As an example, becoming self-actualized is ultimately about rising above and relating to that which is greater than oneself. In its simplest terms, it is a form of "spiritual transcendence"—the realization that we need to accept that we are one small piece of a larger puzzle.

In many ways, I believe the upcoming topic of transcendence can be considered the distant cousin of Maslow's self-actualization. Let me explain what I mean. Self-actualization is indeed a noble and well-intentioned goal of an individual's growth plan and should not be ignored in favor of some newly polished terminology. Yet transcendence can reasonably be considered the "next level" of human development in that it is focused on the growth we intend to accomplish outside of ourselves. As Erich Fromm suggested, for reasons other than our own survival, becoming transcendent makes us care about the things that all of us tend to create.

I do not know where Laz will take this next discussion; however, I believe that he might favor what Erich Fromm proposed. In fact, it appears that there is every reason to believe that with his persistent emphasis on personal responsibility and awareness, Laz has piloted me precisely to this point in the voyage. Honestly, the next logical step that a spiritual guide can give any otherworldly explorer would be to look beyond the reaches of himself or herself.

Bud: You mentioned last time that we were to discuss transcendence—is that correct?

Laz: Yes, reincarnation—going to the next level of existence. For a minute, think about the idea that reincarnation is a form of energy. I hope to capsulize that thought for both of you tonight.

B: Before we start with that, I have one piece of housekeeping that might relate to our discussion tonight. When a soul passes, is it aware of everything or just aware of and processing its most recent, isolated human experiences?

L: Only part of your question is correct or related to tonight's discussion. Actually, as you are living in your human shell, you are experiencing everything that is being learned by the other incarnations that drop from your octopus head. However, whether you are learning from all of that information or even aware of it is difficult to determine.

B: Are you suggesting that we do not extend our learning beyond our own octopus appendages, cluster-soul companion incarnations, or other octopus-head activities?

L: That might be possible if you were an energy that had become "whole"—meaning that you had become highly advanced. Even then, it would take an enormous amount of energy for you to be completely attuned to what the others had learned—you would need to have been blended with them because they are all different life experiences.

B: With highly advanced souls, when information is being passed on from other souls, I would need to be attuned to a similar "soul path" or "mission" in order to absorb anything—would that be correct?

L: Absolutely.

B: I think I understand.

L: Bud, everything is connected. Think, for a moment, if you were able to take every octopus head and hang them all up as they held on to one another with their tentacle legs. You would have created a spiderweb universe of octopuses. If you could do that, you would have learned all that is needed for a soul to achieve—the comprehensive, blended wisdom of all soul knowledge. Now, think of that as being infinite—where everything I just stated is occurring over and over.

B: I think that is where I was going with my initial thoughts—the range of exchanged learning within all incarnations.

L: Yes, each octopus head has an impact on the lifetimes that are involved with the other octopus heads. You would have to be on every tentacle and within every head of every octopus throughout all time—imagine the learning structure that is needed to put that all together. That is the answer to your original question.

B: So, the initial question that I asked was not superficial?

L: No. But realize this: you could only become "all-knowing" by getting through all of the options of all of the octopuses, and if that was ever achieved, then you would have become the one who created them in the first place.

B: Sorry, but you have left me breathless with what you have just said. Can we move on now that you have answered my initial question, and can you give me your ideas on how I should approach transcendence?

L: First, what do you think transcendence is? I would like you to answer that question.

B: Is it simply the process of ascending above—the opportunity for a soul to advance to another, possibly higher, level of existence?

L: Obviously, but you would have to go through many challenges for that to occur. For example, have you lived and experienced life within all the different races, physical environments, mental disciplines, physical handicaps, and so forth? Essentially, it would involve having moved and existed within a multitude of octopuses and octopus heads.

B: In order to transcend and become complete, I need to have experienced that?

L: Yes. If you accomplished that, you could get ready to advance to another dimension or another planetary system—perhaps move beyond the space occupied by humans, ready to start the process all over again.

B: So, as you have suggested in the past, I would have to experience "all things," not just my assigned soul tasks within this lifetime?

L: As I have said many times, it takes a full experience.

B: I'm shocked. How many lives are required to accomplish such a task?

L: It is a transition that can be recycled and, for some, might never end.

B: I am going to assume, for the moment, that some life cycles can be vertical or advancing, whereas others can just be horizontal—in other words, plateauing. Is that right?

L: Yes. But remember your previous learning. Sometimes the creator intervenes and makes the choice of what a soul needs to experience—we have talked about that before. Exclusive vertical-versus-horizontal choices by any soul are actually somewhat rare.

B: Because of what you have just said, is it possible that a soul could "hopscotch" over some learning experiences with a creator's blessing?

L: Very possible, if the creator made that decision. My caution is that it would take a highly advanced soul for the creator to allow that kind of intervention.

B: Laz, before we go any further, I revisited the writings of a psychologist, Abraham Maslow, and his study of the hierarchy of needs. Is your view of a soul's transcendence the same thing? He wrote about a similar vertical development of psychological, social, and self-fulfillment to become self-actualized or transcended.

L: Actually, Bud, one word would cut through all of this and that man's work. Can you tell me what that word is?

B: Could it be *understanding*?

L: It is *awareness*, yes. Now think about how hard it would be to make anyone aware of what we have just discussed and have that person absorb it into his or her soul's development. Basically, each soul has to become aware and learn over and over. Unfortunately, with each life transition something learned is lost. Sadly, there are souls on the "other side" desperate to find what they have lost and left behind. In cases like that, a soul would have to start that portion of the learning all over again—we talked about destabilized energy in previous evenings.

B: Because I have an interest in the treatment of human trauma, is that another example of how that loss might occur, where a portion of a soul is still trapped within some deep trauma in this lifetime?

L: Of course, it could be trapped, and that would affect any transcendence plan. Those souls would not be completed energy and therefore could not start a reincarnation plan. Do you see the problems that start to be created through the absence of awareness?

B: Are you suggesting that if I cannot move through the levels you previously discussed, achieving awareness and moving toward a transcendence plan will be impossible?

L: Correct—but let's talk a bit about current incarnations. Let me share something with you. There are many people or souls who are part of an existing octopus, yet they never reach the head, nor have they experienced completing their energy. Those souls keep moving from tentacle to tentacle, completely unaware of the possibility of joining their remaining energy within the head. They have one human experience after another—over and over—often repeating the same life and never learning anything or developing their soul energy.

Here is a way to examine this. A life on your planet is like going to a university, and the octopus that you reside in is like one of the colleges within that university. There are many different colleges where a soul could study. A soul could study to become a healer or an artist. Perhaps a soul would occupy an octopus head that was dedicated to learning everything that is required to become a teacher. In each of these examples, all of the dropped appendages would be focused on the very specific curriculum of the octopus head—focused on learning everything required within that "college," both the yin and the yang.

B: And the path to transcendence is laid out by completing a soul education in each of these "colleges" and the complete university?

L: It would only be achieved in this fashion. So, if you viewed the spiderweb that we discussed earlier, which has all of the octopus heads attached, each head is a college within the university where souls study.

B: I have one additional thought on all of this. The souls who are stuck on any one of a number of appendages dropped from their octopus head and cycling over and over—are they caught in something that you and I would perceive as negative, such as drug abuse, or could it be something positive?

L: Obviously, it is critical that a soul must become open-minded to move forward as a soul. Unfortunately, there are too many dogmatic groups on your planet that simply do not allow that openness to occur.

Here is an example of what I am talking about. Imagine, for a moment, that you are a blacksmith back in the day of castles and knights, and you are very good at making swords. Then, suddenly, you are reincarnated, again as an artisan, this time with the responsibility to build magnificent structures, but you refuse to do that—you are still making swords in your basement. You have cut off the opportunities to develop within the creative artist portion of the octopus—you cannot graduate from that class within the college. Dogmatic beliefs sometimes cut off the ability to open oneself up to alternative beliefs that could help a soul to complete an appendage.

B: Even though the people around an individual would encourage the new skill set—building structures.

L: Yes. What you might want to consider is that a fair portion of your population is like the blacksmith—simply stuck on an appendage.

B: If that is true, then what motivates a sense of awareness that would allow a soul to advance beyond a particular appendage?

L: Knowing that the knowledge is there to learn and that it is free. Knowing that each lifetime is going to bring more opportunities and more knowledge to develop one's soul.

B: But I have to become aware of everything that you have suggested throughout this afterlife discussion, correct?

L: You cannot be unwilling to be open-minded. It helps to never place yourself in a position where you are cut off from all of your opportunities.

B: On a related matter, regarding the souls that are stuck—do younger souls have a more difficult time grasping this concept of developmental awareness?

L: Not necessarily, because they are still reincarnated with other, more advanced souls around them.

B: If I concluded that a soul was essentially living life on "autopilot," would that soul be less likely to get off the tentacle?

L: Yes, especially if the soul is not open-minded—because it is the open-mindedness that leads to awareness.

B: Help me digest what you are suggesting here. Can you give me three things that would help a human soul become more open-minded and therefore more aware of what is required to advance or transcend?

L: First, seeing worth in themselves. Many look into the mirror and see the same thing every day and have little hope about the possibility of advancing, and this limits their value. Without self-worth or value, they are not going to try something different—they are not going to want to get off the couch and attempt to advance themselves. They just do not feel as though anything is going to go their way.

Second, they need to have competent people around them. People who are willing and able to pull them out of a self-imposed rut. A mentor, of sorts, to show them new things and be willing to help them advance. This is essential because they do not otherwise see new opportunities.

The third thing they need is an association with a healer— someone or something that comes into a human life and supports change. When people become attached to healers, they tend to open up more freely. They become more willing to learn and advance themselves. People need healing advocates, and surprisingly, they come in many forms—animals, humans, or knowledge.

B: Laz, is it possible that an aware or advanced soul could innocently slip and discard some of its learning or awareness? And if so, what could cause something like that to occur?

L: I will share one event with you where the weather on your planet actually caused a healer soul to reverse some of its growth and fall away from its real-life advancement.

B: Excuse me, do you mean the actual physical weather on this planet?

L: Let me explain. There was a soul who had a great healing gift and lived on a beautiful farm. This woman constantly helped people out, and in some cases, she saved people. She eventually studied and became a veterinarian because she loved horses. Caring for these horses became the focus of her life, until lightning struck her barn and killed all of her animals. After that, she became so distraught that she never helped anyone again—the loss of her animals was too much.

The lesson learned was that she was a good person and put a lot into saving the animals, and when the storm came, it took away her purpose of healing others. Your question about slipping is not frivolous—advancing toward transcendence, even with awareness, is a difficult thing for a soul to do.

B: Laz, if a soul is fortunate enough to reach the initial levels of transcendence, what new incarnation choices does it have?

L: It has many—it could choose to become a spiritual guide like myself, or what is referred to as an alternate healer guide, a soul that comes to others, heals them or the situation, and then goes on its way. Actually, there are quite a few of them on your planet—they are the souls that come and save a life when it is not the time for someone to pass over.

B: Can you explain more about the need for a soul to have increased its self-esteem in order to move forward?

L: Again, without it, you do not have the foundation that is necessary to move forward. The ultimate goal is to achieve transcendence. You cannot accomplish that without a clear sense of self.

B: And that gives a soul the availability of unlimited options?

L: And knowledge.

B: Is everything that you have explained a prerequisite to joining with the one who created us?

L: Absolutely—yes. Think of it this way: the path to achieving such a thing is very long. I find it interesting that when a soul passes, it is looking down the barrel of a lengthy process, whereas those remaining on earth simply think that the soul is completely and totally in heaven.

B: With everything that you have stated this evening, I cannot imagine what your responsibilities are like.

L: My responsibility is simple—to bring awareness in an effort to move a soul toward transcendence. My challenge is this: How do you bring awareness to someone who does not know that you exist?

Let me give you some guide secrets. People think that the life in front of them is true awareness. It is really hard to make them understand that what is really going on involves what they do not see, feel, or know.

B: We are off target right now, and I felt that we were very close to the end of an afterlife explanation—do you agree?

L: I think you are right. I also think you should let me write the conclusion when we get together next time.

Shirlet: Bud, this is odd, but he is showing an old-fashioned key and a wreath.

B: Why would he show us these things?

L: Let me tell you why a guide would do something like that—it is because people relate to stories and symbols; that has always been a major part of our journey together. In a discussion of the afterlife, symbols get people through the problems and difficulties while they struggle to understand such a complex issue. I use symbols because most of the people I work with can better relate to what they can see. Having said that, I will explain what both of these symbols mean next time.

Since the conclusion of this evening's discussion, it appears that whenever I try to come to terms with the idea of soul transcendence, the only arm-bending required is that I maintain an exceptional level of unwavering open-mindedness and awareness. Ironically, in making that choice, I will be taking the unanticipated position of abandoning what now appears to be the rubble of my firmly held Buddhist belief of anatman—the concept that began this afterlife voyage.

What I have come to appreciate, however, is this: Laz has carefully arranged a plan for transcendence through his words, his stories, his analogies, and his hoaxes—not with long-winded speechmaking but with a chattiness and clever irony that, despite the strangeness, I have found to be both contagious and, at times, calmly compelling.

Now, however, as I begin to face the conclusion to my afterlife writings, I am left to contend with two remaining questions: First, how do I live a life that is aware and open-minded with respect to a place so unknown as where our souls reside—where would that kind of insight come from? And second, for that matter, even if I am aware, which specific attributes of mindfulness that Laz has advanced are most important to ensure success and soul advancement?

These two remaining questions are vital for any spiritual explorer who is interested in "closing the books" on the actuality of a possible life after death. Unfortunately, I have no firm advice to share with any reader. I am simply left with a lot to think about.

Oddly, during my secluded thoughts, time and again I find myself smiling because I believe Laz is whimsically winking at me as he maps out his version of the unwinding path of soul advancement. He knows that I will be distressed about the detail and complexity of everything he has shared. And how do I know this? Because if the roles were reversed, I feel he would be troubled also.

Laz insists that he would like to write the conclusion to this afterlife review. I feel certain that it will not be a run-of-the-mill commentary. As a matter of fact, he has hinted that he would like to continue with a dialogue to bring a conclusion to our debate. That would be unusual. Historically, Laz has simply verbalized his final opinions. I believe that he has more of a personal plan for me regarding my full understanding of an afterlife. As for me, I am simply curious about the meaning behind the key.

CHAPTER 12

Conclusion

Laz was insistent on writing the conclusion to our discussion of the afterlife voyage. He was equally firm that it would be a personal learning session—not simply a narration by him on what we had covered throughout the year. He further stated that from his viewpoint as my personal guide, it is important for me to understand how this information has a real-time effect on my current life. The following represents his thoughts verbatim.

Laz: First, I understand that everything we have discussed up to this point has been challenging and unusual for you. Second, tonight I need to emphasize and follow up on why awareness is so important.

In order to do that, I would like to ask you a series of personal questions. Every afterlife picture that is painted relates directly back to the soul's current incarnation. Let's begin with that basic understanding.

I would like you to do one thing for me. Think about how

you feel about everything that you have done in this life. Tell me about how you might have been flawed during some moments and how you overcame those moments.

B: Generally speaking, I feel better about this entire journey, and I am not just speaking about the afterlife portion of this adventure.

L: Why have you accepted that position?

B: Because I feel like I am more in control and understand what was behind those moments.

L: If you are now in control of those moments, is being higher than "just better" a realistic possibility for you to achieve?

B: By asking that question, are you suggesting that I have a lack of enthusiasm regarding my life history over time?

L: In a way, yes. But for now, do something else for me: think about how you feel about the "inner you," the part of you that your meditation addresses.

B: I would say that I generally feel more comfortable.

L: Interesting. Are you suggesting that you are, again, being "just better"?

B: Come on, Laz, what are you suggesting here specifically?

That if I am comfortable, then I am not doing the work required to continue with any soul advancement and therefore reducing my ability to modify any afterlife outcomes?

L: OK, if what you say is true, then why would I start the conclusion of this afterlife discussion by asking you these questions?

B: Your expectations are higher than mine?

L: I am suggesting this: you have always been capable of maintaining your entire energy output, including physiological outcomes like your health, aging, and so forth—all the challenges that you face in life.

Now, how do you feel about the start of our conclusion on the afterlife?

B: I am feeling guilty because I have been relaxing here and expecting you to carry the load in formulating this chapter and not anticipating where your questioning was going.

L: What I have been doing is suggesting that control is something that should be looked at internally and not something that is to be used to modify others. It is only through this type of "control" that a focus on a positive afterlife outcome is achieved. When a soul learns to control its own outcome, all the other desires, both while living and in the afterlife, fall into place.

B: Do I fall victim to what you are suggesting because it is easier to project the need for control on issues and concerns that are external to me—essentially, that I have almost a complete disregard for how any of this plays out in an afterlife scenario?

L: Yes, and this is so because an external process is of little value to oneself. Let me explain. Entertain this for a moment—pretend that you have five thousand dollars in your hand right now. Will you throw that money up in the air, or will you control how you go about spending or saving it?

B: Obviously, I will try to control how it is spent.

L: Then why would a soul—or in this case, you—control money but not yourself, especially when your afterlife experience is on the line?

B: Interesting. If I chose to spend the same amount of energy controlling my current life and my soul's development, then all the energy historically spent in trying to control external life issues would simply take care of itself?

L: Yes. You asked me for an end to the book—well, we have started.

B: I get that part, but what is the lesson from this line of questioning?

L: If individuals are willing to control their money, then why would they lose control over their human physiology—their minds, their human shells, the thoughts they have and the actions they take toward themselves and others? That doesn't make much sense to me. All of that is part of your afterlife assessment. You will account for whether you took care of your creation—including how you tried to control others.

B: Is it your intention this evening to ask me these questions as a way to tie them back to what we have discussed up to this point?

L: Somewhat—there are many distractions that you face in an effort to become aware of what is real. For example, assume, for a moment, that life is an illusion, and if you are the programmer or creator of that illusion, then why is the program what it has been for you?

B: Because I chose it?

L: On the surface, yes, but it is much more complex than that. Souls place themselves in any number of precarious situations—associating with bad people and bad places, making indiscriminate choices—and that has an impact on the outcome of what souls eventually experience. There are multiple chaotic choices for every soul life.

B: I am beginning to become skeptical because of what you

have just said. Are you alluding to part of my human experience being "rigged" in some fashion?

L: Even if it is, the human warrior that we discussed would find a way to overcome that. His or her advantage would come with the understanding and awareness of what really happens within an incarnation.

B: Why is this part of our discussion important?

L: Because we are talking about the end of this book.

B: If that is the case, then please explain the meaning behind the key.

L: I already have, and I was hoping that you would have picked up on it—the key has always represented awareness.

B: Help me to understand this better. If my afterlife experience is based on my thoughts and actions while living, then the absence of awareness can be a serious handicap.

L: Without question. Here is something else to consider regarding all of this. Think about the ripple effect involved with the control we have been discussing. Somebody gets controlled by somebody, who gets controlled by somebody, who gets controlled by somebody, etcetera, etcetera—from an afterlife perspective, it will always go back to the need for you to control yourself and not others.

B: In a situation like you just explained, if I am aware of the controlling factors, then the choices I make will be "healthier"?

L: Absolutely.

B: Otherwise, I would be flying blind, correct?

L: Think of this. Say you are walking in the park one day and you see a big wasp nest. Here are your options: you can walk up and kick it, or you can walk away. If you kick it, the wasps will come and get you; plus, they will attack others walking in the park. The result is you in the hospital and others getting stung—notice the ripple effect.

This is what I would like to talk about: the ripple effect of one's actions and how that might affect an afterlife experience. The ripple effect can cause things way beyond the perception of the human mind and, subsequently, a person's life after death.

As an example, the ripple effect of one's actions doesn't just ripple around the one who caused it; it goes on and on—like you had dropped a heavy rock into a lake.

Now, this next part may make you shudder: the ripples don't just appear within this life; the energy ripple of your actions covers all time, including past lives.

B: That is incredible.

L: Try to imagine the devastating effect this can have on an afterlife picture.

B: Are you suggesting that if I create a negative ripple effect in this life, I need to have that balanced out in other times as well?

L: Look at this through the octopus analogy. Think, for a moment, that a big cinder block is about to hit your octopus's head. How would that be? The soul energies—your cluster mates—that have completed their tentacle lives and have made it back to the head of the octopus and thought that they were ready for new incarnations or advancement and were home free. Perhaps they were even contemplating moving on to the next octopus head. Then, suddenly, here comes a cinder block that was delivered because of a ripple effect created from one of the other cluster soul's remaining life tentacles.

B: And that would retard the growth of the energies that were in the head of the octopus?

L: It could knock them back for multiple decades. That is where awareness comes into play—if aware, then those souls would not be on the side where the block was headed.

B: I am at a loss—I have no idea how to explain this.

L: It all has to do with the ripple effect of human actions. You have seen delayed reactions throughout your history as well as in your stress-related illnesses—it is the same thing.

B: Let me stop and ask a question. You are suggesting that human energy can create such a ripple effect, correct? Then is it possible for any accumulated energy to do the same—and would that also affect human afterlife scenarios?

L: Yes. For example, we previously discussed the ability of human thoughts to create forms. These energies could have a negative ripple effect and a subsequent impact on a soul's life and progress.

B: In the bigger picture, is there a required balancing of these issues—essentially creating a yin and yang effect?

L: Not always. Sometimes the positive awareness that we have been discussing creates the balance. Other times, the human warriors have the ability to balance some issues—so it is not always the individual soul's responsibility.

B: I have to believe that the human level of awareness regarding everything that you have shared is extremely low. If that is the case, then I suppose human afterlife reincarnation cycles are very often just repetitive—living the same life scenarios over and over.

L: That is one of the reasons why time keeps repeating itself—many of you are in a loop. Research this if you like; the academic and learned people on your planet have already done this. Your history keeps repeating itself.

B: Starting with the task you gave me in the beginning, is the objective of my incarnation to evolve out of the repetitive cycles of my life plans?

L: The only way to do that is with awareness and control of yourself—so your answer is yes. I'll ask you again: Why give up? Why say you are comfortable with aging and eventually passing when you have the ability to change your life-cycle plans?

B: Is that a plan for everybody and the blueprint to move out of a series of repetitive incarnations?

L: The best way to describe all of this is that it is a maze of human emotions. Think about this: Say you are walking down the street and you see a field, and you decide to walk through it. You are being affected by every person, emotion, and human activity that has ever been present in that field. Think of them as if they were laid out as spiderwebs of emotions.

B: Yet I am unaware of that.

L: Exactly. Your awareness of and even your ability to believe in such an event are not turned on.

B: If I was aware of or could believe in such a situation, what could I do with that awareness?

L: You could connect to those emotions and change the

negatives to positives. Warriors do this all the time. You could essentially change the makeup of that land and the outcome of its future.

B: If that were possible, then the next person to walk through that field would feel the positive aspects of the change?

L: Yes.

B: This is somewhat straying from the afterlife summary, and I would like to ask a question that might take us even further off that path. This ability that you imply is almost Christlike—is that what he possessed?

L: That and much more. And there have been others with the ability to change existing energy fields. They could actually look into the air and see the spiderwebs we have been discussing—that comes with the awareness. During your ancient times, the ability to reconnect energy fields is how people were healed.

B: Are there souls who reincarnate following an afterlife examination and arrive with that level of awareness intact?

L: Yes. But every soul has the opportunity to develop such an awareness. It is unfortunate that the human ego sees it as absurd or bizarre.

Let's rewind this discussion for a moment. If every human

had the willingness to become aware, what state would your planet be in? What afterlife reviews would be taking place, and what new incarnations would be developed? The formula is easy: apply your energy to controlling yourself, not controlling others.

B: Sadly, I think to push such a message would be viewed as "way out there."

L: You are likely accurate with that statement, and what is additionally sad is what is not learned because of that type of reception. Here is something that will really push it "out there"—and it involves the aspect of control that we have been discussing. Compared with humans, trees and flowers do not feel evil or the need to control one another—they are always positive and good and leave each other to their planned existence. And as a result, they are better weather maps than humans—they have longevity beyond humans, and they have feelings of love, connect to each other, and positively contribute to the environment in which they live. I cannot say the same for all of you right now.

What is interesting about this energy discussion and its relationship to the afterlife discussion is this: if you can control more of the energy within the environment and how you perceive it, that is how the energy will also perceive you.

Let's go back to that field we were discussing earlier. It is now the middle of the night; assume, for a moment, that quite a bit of evil activity has taken place in that field. All of that negativity can create havoc with people, or, if you are posi-tive, that energy could start to turn everything around.

B: I am intrigued that having belief and awareness can help balance karma and remove accumulated life bricks.

L: Now, think of the possible changes within your afterlife experience. Development comes in many stages. The biggest development is in understanding what is really around you.

Currently, the human-development pyramid is upside down—people should be controlling themselves, their own personal environment, and attending to the awareness of what they cannot see, not others.

B: Is it vanity to assume that any one of us could change a physical environment?

L: Here is an example to help you understand. If your car broke down, you would take it to a mechanic who knew everything about auto engines. It is not vanity, because he can diagnose and fix your car. He knows what he is doing because he under-stands the problem, and he is aware of what needs to be done.

B: Is it accurate to assume that the mechanic's awareness could be similar to that of any human who is intending to cor-rect a portion of his or her life?

L: Absolutely. Assume, for a moment, that you have become

your own mechanic. When in that state, what are you thinking about your human shell? What would you need fixed? And what mechanisms would you need to modify each flaw? Think of how that would affect your travels through the levels of the aura and senses we discussed earlier.

B: Laz, in deciding to write the conclusion of this book, what did you summarize in your mind as you thought about it?

L: I wanted to make sure that you understood that all human emotions and thoughts go into a form.

B: And how does that directly relate to the afterlife?

L: Because they are all ripple effects that travel through time and space. The ripple effect is what all of you do. Ripple-effect energy doesn't just go around you; it goes through everything, even into death.

Here is a way to process where I am going with this thinking: Why is it that some spirits move on with their mates or to a higher plane of existence within the octopus head, whereas others are haunting a house on your planet for generations? It has everything to do with what happened, the intent of their actions, the awareness of their position, and the ripple effect that caused it all to happen. If this process was not applied, it would not have happened as I just laid it out.

Let me explain it further. For a moment, imagine that a couple wants to purchase a home, but it is in a bad neighborhood. They know that it is not a desirable area, but they really want that house. They go ahead and buy it, and they live there for twenty years. Unfortunately, something bad happens to them, and they are seriously injured during a break-in. Well, the ripple effect started when they decided to buy a home in a troubled area. They were aware but did not care about what they were doing, and the awareness was cut at that second.

Now, when this couple passes from their injuries, because of this ripple effect, they do not roll over to the next tentacle or go to their mates within the head of the octopus to ready themselves for a new incarnation. They are caught in the ripple effect—a loop, if you will—of that property and the impact of the injuries.

Now, this ripple also goes to the people who broke into that home and committed the crime that caused those injuries. They left a thought-form of the attack in that house, and that home is alive with all that negative energy. The individuals who committed this crime go on to commit other crimes, and when they pass, they are also stuck because of the ripple effect. Now there is a whole mess of souls stuck due to the ripple effect that started with one decision—to buy a home in a bad neighborhood.

B: And all of what you just relayed moves through all the levels of the afterlife you discussed previously?

L: Yes.

B: This singular ripple is affecting the senses, auras, heavens and hells, and so forth?

L: One hundred percent. Now, let's take this back to the octopus—which is where you started this journey. This will not be easy to talk about, but I will try to put it all together for you and others.

Assume, for a moment, that your soul has made it to the octopus head, and you are doing well and are ready to make important soul-development decisions for your portion of the energy. Suddenly, one of the tentacles from one of your mates decides to go bananas and commits a horrendous crime. You would feel that, and it would ripple through every other dropped tentacle of the remaining mates and back up to the head, causing all of you great problems.

This one event could bring down the awareness from every energy within the head of the octopus and bring down everyone's vibration. Every energy would be fighting to keep its head above water. They could be plunged into a position where all the energies of the octopus head would have to "relearn" everything.

B: Does an act like that affect a guide like yourself?

L: Of course. It would not affect my position, but I would feel it and have to start over with all the teachings that had been previously understood by everyone within the head of the octopus.

B: You have suggested in the past, however, that any failures within the tentacles of any octopus head are opportunities for learning by all of the mates.

L: And look how much depends on just that—do you now realize the consequences of not being in control of yourself as a soul? Can you tell me what I mean by that?

B: Is it as simple as this—any soul advancement or transcendence is tied to what you have suggested?

L: I believe that you are missing a bigger point. Remember, you are your own creator, and you have your own universe to care for—your organs, your blood vessels, all of your human shell inner workings. Every little piece of energy inside of you is counting on you to be able to care for it and help or intercede to control its environment. It ties back to the accountability that you will be responsible for everything that you have created, loved, and understood. If you are negligent with this, there is the real possibility for things to go off track.

If you need a model to understand this, just look at the conditions on your planet now—that model has the capacity to go on and on if the participating souls do not take control of their individual internal and external chaos.

B: I do not know how to respond to that—it is way beyond my pay grade.

L: Whatever you feed yourself and how you believe are attuned by you and you will be held responsible for that plan. It is your individual world that you live in and have created, and you must decide whether you are going to allow it to become a renegade environment. You absolutely must think about this before your afterlife begins; otherwise, you could get caught in a number of levels of your review.

All that we have discussed has always been within your control—it is the attention paid to controlling others that deflects a soul's energy away from its internal awareness and final responsibilities.

B: Laz, what are some of your final thoughts?

L: I told you what the key represented—awareness—but I did not tell you what the wreath represented. To be candid, it has everything to do with the octopus analogy that we have discussed. It is a symbol; it is a circle; it represents eternity—it never ends.

B: Are you referring to the continuation of life—that a singular soul moves throughout the spiderweb of incarnations and octopus heads?

L: You are living energy, and as such, the purpose of that energy is to continue to be and exist. Everything recycles—always—including the universe that you occupy.

Your scientists continue to look for the beginning. The

answer to their question is that all of you are the beginning and the end. Energy has always existed, it just re-forms. Within that context, everything that was known is experienced by a human soul, and that continues throughout all time.

Bud, you are part of an ongoing energy—you are not just out there running into things. The energy that makes up your soul is more advanced than you or anyone can imagine.

Let me share this example with you. Go back to the field we were discussing earlier and know that if you walked up to a flower that was budding in the middle of that field, your energy could become that flower and fully understand its existence, yet still remain attached to your human shell. You have the capacity to experience all life that way. It is your human ego that tells you that this is impossible, and as a result, your soul awareness is silenced. The end result, unfortunately, is that you look to control others and the environments surrounding both yourself and them.

You shared with me that this afterlife journey started with trying to understand and resolve your conflict with the Buddhist doctrine of anatman. You wondered why such a doctrine would exist. Now you know that the greatest deterrent in trying to understand your Buddhist puzzle has always been you. Your conflict is twofold—a concentration on your external control of others (no self) and, more importantly, an absence of true soul awareness (no soul).

Finally, your Buddhist friend Khenchen is a wise man and was correct when he suggested to you that within silence, you will find the answers to your life questions. In the case of the

afterlife, they are simple—controlling your internal environment and developing your soul's awareness.

Although Laz has written an appealing and somewhat encourag-
ing ending to my afterlife excursion, I have a few final thoughts
on the deepest of all mysteries; what happens to me when I die.

There have been many challenging moments throughout
this voyage, surprisingly however as I reviewed my historical notes, the singular comment that reverberates is the following: *"stagnation only comes with the human shell, and
when that occurs, the human ego takes over stalling out the
soul."* We seem to rely on our ego for support and strength
while developing our overall earthly plan and self-esteem, yet
Laz suggest that meaningful *"soul awareness"* can only be
achieved when the human ego is silenced. Why does this barrier occupy such a significant position in every human soul's
development?

Whenever I visit my Buddhist friends, they interpret the
effects of the human ego as a cruel dictatorship that is on a
tireless mission to suspend the development of the human
mind. Each time we discuss this topic, they feel comfortable
in defending any ill-treatment directed against the human
ego—especially if by doing so it can release its authority over
how we live.

I have to believe that every psychological professional I
have worked with would be shaking his or her head in disbelief

with what I have just suggested. So, for the record let me try to represent what they are likely to recommend. In principle, my colleagues would propose that the ego is simply a cluster of activities and not a singular item to be attacked—claiming that the human ego is a function of the mind. And their predictable reaction to the Buddhist approach of anatman? An absent human ego, coupled with the reduction of a sense of self, would be an unmitigated disaster.

This yearlong adventure into the afterlife realm has been revolutionary for me, and I am sure there are more sleepless nights that remain. For now, however, I continue to be preoccupied with the Buddhist doctrine of anatman and how it relates to this debate about the human ego and subsequently my afterlife experience. Let me explain in more detail how I might continue to resolve this conundrum in the future.

There are several authors that I follow on a regular basis, and Michael Pollan is one of my favorite. I was fascinated with *The Omnivore's Dilemma* and *Cooked*, but for this discussion I would like to reference his latest book—*How to Change Your Mind*.

In short, his latest work dives into both the history and the author's personal experiences with the documented psilocybin (magic mushrooms) investigations. Of note is the controlled clinical experimentation and how it appeared to *freeze* the human ego. In essence, there was an *awareness* explosion that occurred, allowing for an unpolluted and powerful view of one's existence. Throughout Pollan's record of events, he sketches an interruption of one's ego followed by the merging of oneself with nature and the universe—a mystical experience that seemed to shift a person's perspective and priorities.

What I found strange in revisiting this highly researched piece of nonfiction was how similar the results linked up to what Laz was privately suggesting during his conclusion narrative. Over and over there seemed to be a comparative shifting from an external life control to an internal life examination that force-fed a new profound state of awareness.

In addition to this curious alignment with my soulful friend's final recommendations, I was amazed by the individuals who were part of this testing, including the former Apple CEO, Steve Jobs. Upon reading about his experimentation, and being aware of his Buddhist background, I was left with this predicament: Would a professed belief in the Buddhist doctrine of anatman (no self/no soul) have deflated his idea of a human ego, or could the psychedelic experience of psilocybin simply verify its impact by allowing for the opening of his mind and the creation of extraordinary *awareness*—the open-minded awareness shared by Laz?

In an odd way, my conclusion of the existence of an afterlife mirrors the cycles of unexpected change that we all experience in life. Let me explain that comment in more detail. There are many rigid interpretations of how our existence might continue, including the option that it does not advance beyond this life. What is hard to recover from, however, is the possibility that human energy, regardless of its configuration and without warning, could splinter, recycle, and re-form.

I was told what happens to my consciousness as my soul

ruptures and wanders off into the complex world of multiple senses and chakra levels. What troubles me is how my ego administers that information. Without hesitation it becomes defensive and starts to define my afterlife voyage as a configuration of twisting energy fragments mysteriously zigzagging throughout the spirit world looking for a place to land.

As a final point and a question for future discussions - if there is a percentage of my total energy presently resting within the head of the octopus and incarnating on remaining octopus tentacles, then when all of this energy arrives together, who will I be?

Buddhist monks have a term they use in describing the foundation of contemplative therapy—it's known as *brilliant sanity*. It outlines who I am no matter what I am feeling at a particular moment. This unique expression begins to describe the "core" of my being—my most natural state. Perhaps this condition describes the makeup of my human energy when all foreseen incarnations are complete and I become an all-inclusive energy—I would like to think so because I can live with that.

Maybe my Buddhist friend Khenchen was right when he suggested that I have the type of personality that requires charts, maps, and navigational GPS to find my answers. That the details of life and death are inborn within traditional Western truth-seeking teachings. He privately signaled that understanding the doctrine of anatman requires a dedicated return toward meditative breathing. That ultimately my approach and concentration toward breath would uncover how all energy continues, including mine.

ABOUT THE AUTHOR

Bud Megargee is a former senior health-care executive; a Washington, DC, health-care lobbyist; and an independently published, award-winning author. He began writing after exploring Eastern philosophy and alternative medicine techniques in the professional treatment of emotional challenges at a Taiwanese Buddhist monastery.

Mr. Megargee has served as the CEO of Megargee Healthcare Group, specializing in developing behavioral health medical integration and transformation strategies, and is now living in the beautiful green countryside of southeastern Pennsylvania.

You can visit Mr. Megargee at budmegargee.com.

OTHER BOOKS BY THE AUTHOR

Dirt, TRUTH, Music and Bungee Cords:
Conversations with the Souls Who Guide My Life
(CreateSpace, 2015)

Soul Sins and Regrettable Lies
(CreateSpace, 2016)

Soul Mechanics: Unlocking the Human Warrior
(CreateSpace, 2017)

Soul Imprints: The Legacy of Existence
(CreateSpace, 2018)

ABOUT THE ORACLE

Shirlet Enama was born in California and has quietly retained a small, exclusive psychic/oracle practice in the rural, mountainous region of Berwick, Pennsylvania. She attracted the attention of a Buddhist monastery at a young age, and monks who considered her a child of light encouraged her ability to recognize and openly communicate with otherworldly energies, irrespective of their vibration level or dimension of origin. Regarded as a seer by her unearthly partners, she channels personal soul guides in a comfortable and conversational manner and instructs that the explanations shared are the measured moments of one's life voyage, not a forecast of events to come.

In the role of a practitioner of spiritual voice channeling, Shirlet sits quietly when engaged in casual conversation. There is a gentle and simple calmness to the way in which she presents herself, and that stillness carries over while channeling spirit voices from the other side.

For instance, while she is engaged in spirit-channeling dialogue, there is only a slight noticeable change in voice inflection as she rapidly repeats what is exchanged between her and the channeled spirit. She often describes it as a high-speed computer connection.

For more information about Shirlet and her private practice, contact www.Shirlet.com.

Made in the USA
Monee, IL
10 December 2021

84744155R00135